patchwork-play
QUILTS

make the most of scraps, spare parts, and leftovers

Lynn Roddy Brown

Martingale®
& COMPANY

Dedication

To all the families who, in a time of great sorrow, make the unselfish decision to save lives through organ donation

Acknowledgments

The following quilters have generously shared quilts, blocks, and the perfect blue striped fabric. Thank you to: Elizabeth (Liz) Broussard, Denise Goodman, Nona Hoecker, Janice Thompson, Frances (Fran) Urquhart, and Sandra Weaver.

Thanks also go to the Piecemakers of Bellaire United Methodist Church for great quilting advice as well as love and support. Our Friday afternoons are very special.

I would like to thank the staff at Martingale & Company for doing your jobs so well. Special thanks go to editors Karen Costello Soltys, Tina Cook, and Ellen Pahl for so graciously putting up with me.

Finally, thanks to my husband, Bill, for color consultations, photography, box packing, and patience. You have been there for me through good times and bad for over 40 years. I could not ask for a better husband.

Credits

President & CEO: Tom Wierzbicki
Editor in Chief: Mary V. Green
Managing Editor: Tina Cook
Developmental Editor: Karen Costello Soltys
Technical Editor: Ellen Pahl
Copy Editor: Sheila Chapman Ryan
Design Director: Stan Green
Production Manager: Regina Girard
Illustrator: Laurel Strand
Cover & Text Designer: Shelly Garrison
Photographer: Brent Kane

Mission Statement

Dedicated to providing quality products and service to inspire creativity.

Patchwork-Play Quilts: Make the Most of Scraps, Spare Parts, and Leftovers
© 2011 by Lynn Roddy Brown

That Patchwork Place® is an imprint of Martingale & Company®.

Martingale & Company
19021 120th Ave. NE, Ste. 102
Bothell, WA 98011-9511 USA
www.martingale-pub.com

Printed in China
16 15 14 13 12 11   8 7 6 5 4 3 2 1

Library of Congress Cataloging-in-Publication Data is available upon request.

ISBN: 978-1-60468-037-9

CONTENTS

INTRODUCTION

I started the schoolhouse quilt shown here in 1991 in a class taught by Trudy Hughes. The photograph in her book showed red schoolhouses on a white background. I selected a solid red, a tone-on-tone white, a tone-on-tone blue, and an almost-interesting red print. At that point in my quiltmaking career, I could not imagine doing anything different. This simple quilt has strong graphic appeal but no surprises. Looking at one corner of the quilt tells the entire story. There are no unusual fabrics, alternate patterns, or diagonal lines.

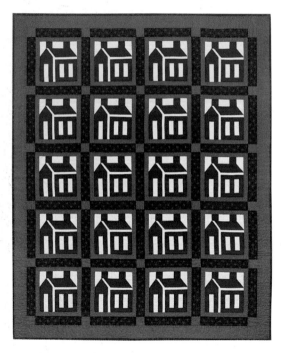

I started this quilt in a class taught by Trudie Hughes in 1991. Since all of the Schoolhouse blocks in the quilt were identical, I cut them all at the same time. I didn't finish this quilt, however, until 2002. It measures 57" x 72".

As I continued on my quiltmaking journey, scrap quilts with many fabrics became more appealing. The never-ending designs that could be created using a few easy-to-piece units fascinated me. Simple patches—squares, rectangles, and triangles—when combined could create complex and exciting quilts. By changing the value placement, the type of fabric, or the color of the blocks, I could create many different-looking quilts using the same blocks or units. The possibilities were endless.

After taking classes, studying hundreds of quilts, and much trial and error, I learned to make scrap quilts that pleased me by applying my own set of rules. I used very consistent values and scattered colors evenly across the quilt surface. I often made quilts that used all the same types of fabrics, such as 1930s reproduction prints, or two colors, such as pink and brown. My rules worked for me.

Then one day I saw an antique pinwheel quilt that I fell in love with. It didn't follow any of my rules. The values in the quilt were inconsistent. The same pink fabric was used in many blocks and it often touched the same pink in other blocks. The pinwheels turned in opposite directions. A few of the blocks were made using half-square-triangle units that didn't form pinwheels. After analyzing the quilt, I realized that the inconsistent value placements created alternate patterns. I saw Hourglass and Broken Dishes blocks as well as Pinwheels. Areas of light and dark along with the color concentrations in some areas blurred the block outlines, creating additional patterns.

Scrap quilts may be simple, very complex, or anywhere in between. It's up to the individual quiltmaker to decide what she finds most pleasing. The next step is understanding how to achieve the desired level of complexity. I've found that the more I understand something the more appreciation I have for it. My eldest daughter and I were given tickets to a symphony performance. Our ears were never trained to appreciate classical music, and we left at intermission. When non-quilters enter my house, they often gravitate toward the simple quilts, those that have a clearly defined pattern. They are easy for the untrained eye to appreciate.

Twenty years ago, my own untrained eyes would never have given that wonderful antique pinwheel quilt a second glance. It's my hope that this book will help other quilters learn more about scrap quilts and gain a greater understanding of and appreciation for them along the way.

When I look at this antique quilt, my eye is constantly moving. My version of this quilt, "Pinwheels Revisited," is on page 24.

understanding
SCRAP QUILTS:
from simple to complex

In all of life we are searching for order. Some of us need more than others. Patchwork quilts have various levels of order or structure. In most, fabrics are pieced into blocks, and then joined together to make a quilt top. A less obvious or more complex structure often results in a more intriguing quilt. If the structure is too complex, however, the pattern may become random and lack a focal point. A simple structure may be too predictable and as a result boring to some viewers. As a quiltmaker, you must decide the level of complexity that you find most pleasing. Many quilters make scrap quilts that they don't like—but they don't understand why. With understanding, you'll be able to create the scrap quilt you have in mind.

When my great-grandmother made quilts, she used leftover scraps from clothing construction. I, however, buy cotton fabric specifically for the quilts I make. Are my quilts scrap quilts? What makes one quilt "scrappier" than another? After 20 years of studying and making scrap quilts, I think I have a few of the answers.

Number of Fabrics

Most quilters would agree that using many fabrics, with varied patterns and colors, is what helps define a quilt as scrappy. The size and shapes of the pieces along with the repetitive use of fabrics also makes a difference.

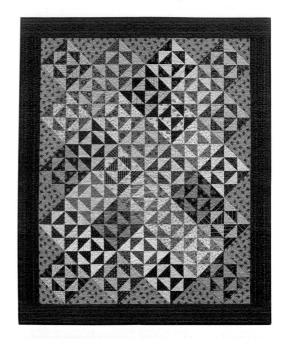

Each block in "Shattered Dishes" (top) uses two fabrics that are repeated eight times. "Crow's Nest" (bottom) blocks have 21 different fabrics, smaller pieces, and three different shapes. "Crow's Nest" is much scrappier.

Value, Value, Value

In most quilts, the outline of the shapes is determined by color. Scrap quilts use many different fabrics in a wide range of colors. It's the relative darkness or lightness of the colors, or value, that determines the pattern.

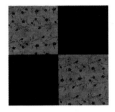 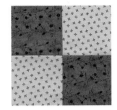

Shown here are two blocks, each using the same pink fabric. In the first block, the pink is lighter than the burgundy. In the second, the same pink is darker than the white-with-red print.

The position of the light and dark pieces is reversed in these blocks. When placed next to each other, the blocks create a secondary checkerboard pattern.

If the placement of value is varied, blocks with the same patches may appear to be different blocks. This use of value, whether planned or not, can be seen in many antique quilts. The Windmill blocks shown below use the same three fabrics with very different results.

Even though these blocks look very different, they all use the same fabrics.

Value differences within a piece of fabric also create patterns. This is called visual texture. Stripes, dots, plaids, vines, and florals are examples of textured fabric. I like my quilts to have a variety of visual textures that can be seen from a distance.

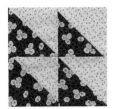  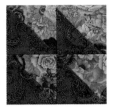

The Little Cedar Tree blocks shown here were each made with two fabrics. In the first, a very light is combined with a dark red. The strong contrast creates a clear pattern. The second block pairs a large light/medium floral with dark brown. The three values in this block provide strong visual texture and a less distinct pattern, resulting in a very scrappy block. The third example has very blurred lines caused by similar colors and textures. The pattern in this block will probably be lost when sewn into a quilt and viewed from a distance.

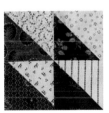  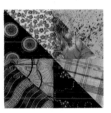

From left to right, the blocks are arranged from the least scrappy to the most scrappy. Eight different fabrics were used in each. The first block pairs shirtings with Civil War reproduction prints. These fabrics have slightly varied visual textures and colors and very consistent values. The second block has inconsistent values and more varied fabrics for a scrappier look. In the third example, the very strong visual textures and inconsistent values are the approach to use if you are trying to make a very scrappy quilt.

LYNN SAYS:
GUILT-FREE FABRIC STASH

With no apology, I confess to owning a huge fabric stash. If I used up my stash, I would no longer have it to play with in wonderful, creative ways. My fabric collection provides inspiration and endless possibilities.

First: least scrappy. Checkerboard pattern, consistent values, very little visual texture.

Second: more scrappy. Checkerboard pattern, inconsistent values, some visual texture.

Third: most scrappy. No defined pattern, inconsistent values, lots of visual texture.

At left:

I used 3" nine-patch units from a block swap to make the three larger blocks. Nine Patch blocks usually come two ways. Blocks with five dark squares are called X blocks and those with four dark squares are called O blocks. When you alternate the X and O units, checkerboard patterns form. In the first block, I used units with strong contrasts in value. The second block has inconsistent values and more visual texture. In the third block, I placed the units randomly. After making the blocks, I pinned them on the design wall and sat in my chair with a cup of tea. I could instantly see a very clear checkerboard pattern in the first block. When my eye moved to the second block, there was more for my mind to sort. The inconsistent values make the individual units more visible. The stronger visual textures add interest. The checkerboard pattern is present but not as obvious. The third block does not form a checkerboard. The randomly placed units with inconsistent values create alternate patterns. My eyes will not stop moving when I view this block. It's my favorite!

Palette

Palette is defined as a range of colors used by an artist. In quilts, fewer color choices usually indicate a more controlled, less scrappy quilt.

In "Hot Stars Over Texas" (page 57), I used just five colors: red, yellow, black, gray, and white. Varying the patterns and shades of each color makes the quilt visually rich.

The reds in "Hot Stars Over Texas" range from tangerine to deep scarlet, and each print is distinctly different from the others.

Common or Related Fabrics

Selecting related fabrics—fabrics that are similar in style and/or color—can make a quilt less scrappy but easier for a beginning scrap quilter to reproduce. The Civil War reproductions fabrics in "Shattered Dishes" (page 47) are an example of related fabrics. If you don't have a large stash, I suggest buying fat quarters of your favorite fabric type as a way to add variety.

"Baby Blue Buckeye" (page 92) uses what I refer to as related fabrics—in this case, 1930s reproduction prints—with a common background.

LYNN SAYS: COLLECTING FABRIC

Fat quarters (approximately 18" x 21") are an easy way to get a large variety of colors and textures while making your fabric budget go further. Sometimes they are sold in coordinated bundles tied together with beautiful ribbons. If you have some of these bundles that have been sitting around for more than a year waiting for a special project, I suggest separating them and using them in scrap quilts. I only buy bundles if they are a group of related fabrics, such as shirtings or 1930s reproduction prints.

quiltmaking TECHNIQUES

In this section I've included some of my favorite techniques and helpful hints. If you're new to quilting, be sure to read through this section. Even if you're an experienced quilter, you may want to try some of the piecing strategies that I use to help ensure that my blocks are accurate and will fit together to create a nicely pieced, square quilt top.

All of the quilts in this book are machine pieced using straight seams and an accurate ¼" seam allowance. All cutting measurements include the seam allowances.

Pinning for Accurate Matching

I pin all places where seam lines or points meet. I often start with a pin pushed straight through these points. I hold this "positioning pin" perpendicular to the fabric, and then place pins on each side.

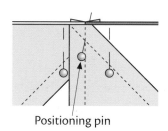

Positioning pin

Units with seam allowances pressed to one side, in opposite directions, can easily be matched. Make certain the opposing seams are pushed tightly together—butted—and then pin.

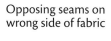

Opposing seams on wrong side of fabric

Accurate match on right side of fabric

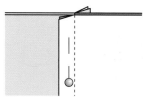

When two half-square-triangle units are joined, the opposing seams are diagonal. For more accurate piecing, I start sewing where the diagonal seams meet.

Begin sewing.

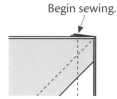

Pressing

After sewing each seam, press it flat as it was sewn to set the seam; then press the seam allowances open or to one side before adding the next piece. Usually seam allowances are pressed to one side, toward the darker fabric. In the project instructions, I suggest that you press many of the seam allowances open. I do this because I machine quilt all my quilts, and pressing the seam allowances open creates a smoother, flatter surface with less skipping and thread breakage. I use quilting patterns that cross over the seams, thereby stabilizing and holding them together. If you're planning to outline the quilt patches either by hand or machine—or if you're planning to tie the quilt—you might want to press all the seam allowances to the side.

Paired Fabrics

I've found an efficient and accurate way to cut and piece units. For many of the quilts in this book, you'll be instructed to pair up your fabrics before cutting. The method is called paired fabrics. With this method, bias edges will be "stuck" together with spray starch and will be stabilized before cutting and sewing.

1. Using the two fabrics that will be sewn together (as directed in the specific project), lay the first fabric, right side up, on the ironing board. Spray evenly with spray starch.

2. Lay the second fabric, right side down, on top of the first, aligning the edges, and press well until dry. The fabrics should now be smooth, crisp, lightly stuck together, and ready to cut.

Half-Square-Triangle Units

I begin with paired squares of fabric to make either two or eight identical half-square-triangle units at once. I always make half-square-triangle units slightly oversized, and then trim them to the correct size.

SQUARES FOR HALF-SQUARE-TRIANGLE UNITS

To determine the size to cut squares, use these formulas:

- **Two identical half-square triangles:** Add 1¼" to the desired finished size and cut your original squares to that size. (For 3" half-square-triangle units, cut two squares, 4¼" x 4¼".)

- **Eight identical half-square triangles:** Add 1¼" to the desired finished size and multiply by two; cut your original squares to that size. (For 3" half-square-triangle units, cut two squares, 8½" x 8½".)

Making Two Identical Half-Square-Triangle Units

1. Make paired fabrics as described in "Paired Fabrics" (page 10). Cut the square in half on the diagonal using a ruler and rotary cutter.

2. Sew the diagonal seams. Press to set the seams, and then press the seam allowances toward the darker fabric.

3. Trim the units, referring to "Squaring Up Triangle Units" (page 12).

Making Eight Identical Half-Square-Triangle Units

1. Make paired fabrics as described in "Paired Fabrics" (page 10). Cut the square in half on the diagonal using a ruler and rotary cutter. Sew the diagonal seams.

2. Align a ruler with the line of stitching and the triangle point. Cut. Repeat for both units to make four triangles.

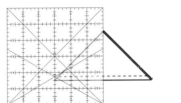

3. Start at the right-angle corner of each of the units from step 2 and stitch the unsewn edge as shown. The stitches will cross at the corner.

Make 4.

4. Align a ruler with the unsewn edge and the point of the units from step 3; cut as shown. You'll have eight identical half-square triangles. Press to set the seams, and then press the seam allowances toward the dark fabric.

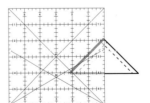

Make 8.

5. Trim the units, referring to "Squaring Up Triangle Units" on page 12.

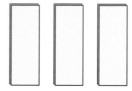

Squaring Up Triangle Units

1. Use a small, square ruler with a diagonal line to trim and square up each half-square triangle. Position the diagonal line on the seam of the unit with the fabric extending just beyond the edge of the ruler. Trim the two adjacent sides.

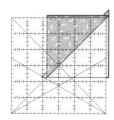

2. Rotate the unit and position the ruler so that the two trimmed edges of the unit are on the ruler lines for the required size. Trim the excess fabric from the remaining two sides.

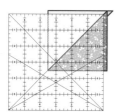
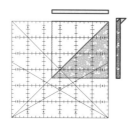

Nine Patch Blocks from Paired Fabrics

You can quickly and easily make two Nine Patch blocks from paired squares of fabric. The two blocks will have opposite placement of the dark and light values. You'll have one X block (a block with five dark squares) one O block (with four dark squares).

X block   O block

1. Cut squares the size needed for your project, or see the table (page 13). Pair the two fabrics to be sewn together as described in "Paired Fabrics" (page 10). Straighten the left edge with a ruler and rotary cutter. Cut three identical segments in the required width.

2. Sew one long edge of *two* of the paired strips. Press toward the dark fabric.

3. Separate the third segment into two strips. Alternating colors, sew one strip to each of the sewn pairs from step 2. Press toward the dark fabric.

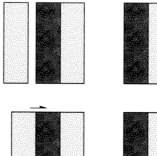

4. Rotate the strip units, trim the left side of each unit, and crosscut three segments from each as shown.

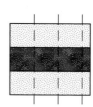
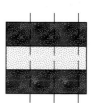

5. Arrange the segments to create two Nine Patch blocks. Sew the seams and press the seam allowances as shown.

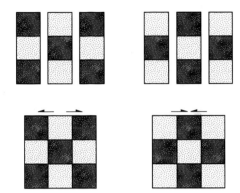

CUTTING SQUARES FOR NINE PATCH BLOCKS

Finished Size	Size of Squares to Cut Cut 1 each of dark and light.	Width of Segments
3"	5"	1½"
4½"	6½"	2"
6"	8½"	2½"

Blocks from Strip Sets

Sewing strip sets is a shortcut for making simple blocks such as the Nine Patch, Four Patch, and Rail. I like to make strip sets from strips that are about 21". This gives more variety, but still has the advantage of quick piecing. Cutting strips from the full width of the fabric results in 42" strips, which can be easily cut in half. A fat quarter, also known as a quilter's quarter, measures approximately 18" x 21" and a fat eighth measures 9" x 21". You can cut strips from both of these cuts as well.

The following chart includes the information you need to make three different sizes of Nine Patch, Four Patch, and Rail blocks from 21" strips. If the quilt you've chosen needs fewer units, the extra blocks will give you a head start on your next project.

MAKING BLOCKS FROM 21" STRIPS

Block	Finished Size	Strip Width	Strips to Cut	Segment Width	# of Blocks
Nine Patch	3"	1½"	3 light, 3 dark	1½"	8 + 2 extra segments
	4½"	2"	3 light, 3 dark	2"	6 + 2 extra segments
	6"	2½"	3 light, 3 dark	2½"	5 + 1 extra segment
Rail	3"	1½"	3 total	3½"	5
	4½"	2"	3 total	5"	4
	6"	2½"	3 total	6½"	3
Four Patch	3"	2"	1 light, 1 dark	2"	5
	4"	2½"	1 light, 1 dark	2½"	4
	6"	3½"	1 light, 1 dark	3½"	2 + 1 extra segment

Making Nine Patch Blocks from Strip Sets

1. Using three medium/dark strips and three light strips, make two strip sets as shown. Press the seam allowances toward the medium/dark. Cut each strip set into segments.

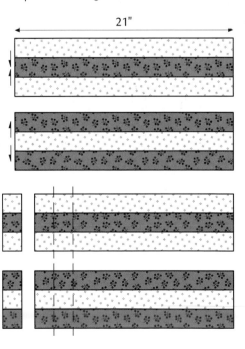

2. Arrange the segments into X blocks and O blocks. Pin and sew the segments together, matching seams. Press the seam allowances as shown.

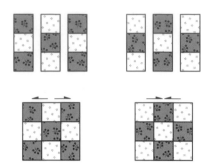

Making Rail Blocks from Strip Sets

Using three strips in the value combinations required by the quilt you have chosen, make a strip set. Press the seam allowances to one side. Trim and square up the left edge of each strip set; cut into segments.

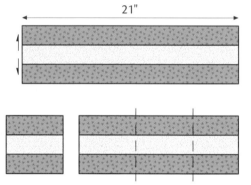

21"

Making Four Patch Blocks from Strip Sets

1. Sew a light strip to a medium/dark strip along the long sides; press toward the medium/dark fabric. Cut the strip set into segments.

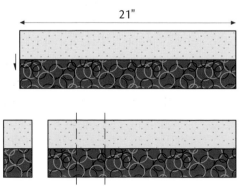

21"

2. Pair the segments and place them right sides together with seams butting. Use straight pins to secure the seams. Sew and press the seam allowances open.

Quarter-Square Triangles

For quarter-square triangles, cut squares twice diagonally as shown. These triangles have the straight grain along their long edges. The short sides are on the bias. When used as side setting triangles, the straight grain is on the outside of the quilt, which helps keep the quilt from stretching.

To make quarter-square-triangle units, I usually sew a half-square-triangle unit and cut it diagonally. This will give you two mirror-image units made of quarter-square triangles. This unit is used in "Shattered Dishes" (page 47) and "The Broken Path" (page 50).

Making Four Identical Three-in-a-Square Triangle Units

The blocks in "Texas Windmills" (page 53) and "Hot Stars Over Texas" (page 57) require four identical units made of one half-square triangle and two

QUILTMAKING TECHNIQUES

quarter-square triangles. I call these three-in-a-square triangle units.

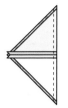

1. Two identical squares are required for the large triangles. The smaller triangles each use one square. For the patterns in this book all of the squares are cut 5½" for a unit that finishes at 4".

2. Spray the two squares to be used as the larger triangles with starch and press until dry. Cut both in half diagonally.

Make 4.

3. Referring to "Paired Fabrics" (page 10) use the two remaining squares to make paired fabrics. Cut into quarters diagonally to yield four pairs of quarter-square triangles.

 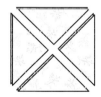

4. Place the paired quarter-square triangles so that the correct fabric is on the top, as instructed in the project directions. The wrong side of the same fabric in all four units should be facing up. Stitch from the corner to the point on the right edge of each triangle pair. Set the seams and carefully press open. Remember you're dealing with stretchy bias edges.

 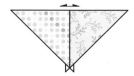

5. Place a unit from step 4 right sides together on a large triangle. Align the long edges and center the smaller pieced unit. Pin. Stitch along the edge. Press toward the larger triangle.

6. Using a Bias Square® ruler, carefully align the diagonal marking on the ruler with the short center seam on the unit. The 4½" marks on each edge of the ruler should align with the long diagonal seam. Trim the right side and the top with a rotary cutter. Rotate the block 180° and cut the remaining two sides so that the block measures 4½" x 4½".

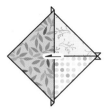

Trim to 4½" x 4½".

Square-in-a-Square Units

Square-in-a-square units have a center square with a triangle attached to each of the four sides, resulting in a second, larger pieced square. Units are much more accurate if the triangles are cut oversized, added to the four sides of the square, and then trimmed.

1. Fold the triangles in half right side out and lightly press to mark the center of each long side. Fold the block in half with right side in and press the edges to mark the centers. Fold the block the opposite way right side in and mark the center of the other two block edges. Use the creases to align a triangle with the center of each block edge. Sew triangles to two opposite sides of the block. Press the seam allowances toward the

triangles and trim the triangle points even with the side of the square.

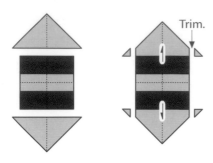

2. Sew triangles to the remaining sides. Press toward the triangles.

3. Place the pieced unit under a square ruler. Align the ¼" line on the ruler with the top and right points of the center square. Trim the right side and top of the block. Rotate the block 180° and trim the two remaining sides in the same manner.

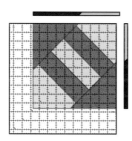 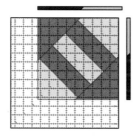

Quilt Settings

A quilt setting or set is how the blocks in a quilt are arranged. The quilts in this book are set in one of four different ways—straight, medallion, diagonal, or in vertical rows (also called a strippy setting). You can always choose a different setting from the one shown in the photograph.

Whenever there are sashing strips or plain alternate blocks in a quilt setting, I suggest that you wait until all the blocks are sewn before cutting those elements of the quilt. Your blocks may vary from the exact size by ⅛" or more due to slight differences in cutting and piecing. Measure your blocks, and then cut those pieces to fit your blocks. Your quilt will go together much easier this way.

Straight Sets

In straight sets, blocks are simply sewn together into horizontal rows. The rows are joined to complete the top. When joining the rows, be sure to carefully match the vertical seams of each row with the next. I pin all of these intersections.

Medallion Sets

Medallion settings feature a central block or focal area, usually with multiple borders. "Broken Dishes Medallion" (page 34) and "Hourglass and Rail Surprise" (page 66) are examples of medallion sets.

Diagonal Sets

Blocks placed on point create diagonal settings. These require side setting triangles and corner setting triangles. Throughout the project instructions, the side and corner setting triangles are cut oversized. This allows for minor piecing variations and gives you an extra margin of insurance, allowing you to trim and square up your quilt after the triangles are added.

1. Sew the blocks together in diagonal rows, adding the side setting triangles to the ends. To add the side setting triangles, first align the corners. Allow the point of the triangle to extend beyond the block as shown. Sew the seam, press toward the triangle, and then trim the point. Sew the diagonal rows together. Add the corner triangles last.

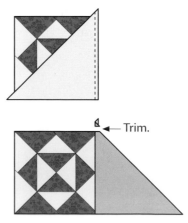

2. Trim the edges of the quilt top ¼" away from the block points before adding borders. Align the ¼" mark of a rotary ruler on the block points as shown.

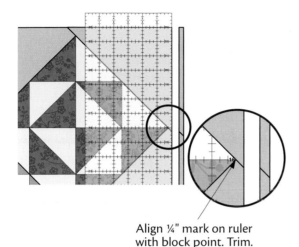

Align ¼" mark on ruler with block point. Trim.

Vertical Strippy Sets

Blocks in this setting are sewn together into panels to create vertical rows. Any number of alternate vertical rows can be included, pieced or unpieced. "Texas Windmills" (page 53) and "Zigzag Cedars" (page 38) are examples of strippy sets.

Borders

When quilts have an unpieced outer border that is wider than 3", I like to cut it on the lengthwise grain. This requires more fabric, but has the advantage of being less stretchy than the crosswise grain. Borders cut on the lengthwise grain help keep the quilt square and flat. The inner borders are cut from the crosswise grain and are sewn together end to end, with a straight or diagonal seam, to get the required length. I prefer a diagonal seam because I think it's less noticeable. If I use a striped fabric, I match the stripe and join the strips with a straight seam. Press all border seam allowances open, whether they are straight or diagonal.

FUSSY CUTTING STRIPES

To fussy cut a lengthwise stripe, first study the fabric to find one stripe or a combination of stripes that will approximately equal the desired width of your border. When you've selected the stripe, add a ¼" seam allowance to each side. Lay the ¼" line of a rotary ruler on the line of the stripe you're using. Cut one layer at a time. Using a short ruler and realigning often seems to work best. Turn the fabric and add a ¼" seam to the other edge of the stripe.

When sewing the fabric to the quilt, place the striped fabric on top. You should be able to see the stripe on the wrong side of the fabric. Use the line in the fabric as a sewing line. It's more important visually to follow the stripe so that it won't be wavy or cut off on the right side of the quilt.

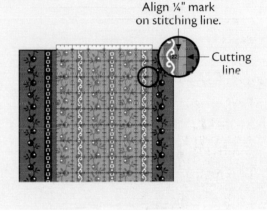

Align ¼" mark on stitching line.

Cutting line

Borders with Butted Corners

1. Lay the quilt out on a smooth surface. Measure lengthwise through the middle. Use this measurement to cut side borders. Mark the middle and quarter points of the borders.

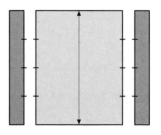

Measure center of quilt, top to bottom.

2. Place the borders on the quilt, right sides together, matching the ends, quarter points, and middle. Pin carefully. If the edges of the quilt have stretched so that they're longer than the borders, take the quilt top, with the pinned border attached, to the ironing board. With the border underneath and the quilt on top, use a steam iron until the quilt can be eased to fit the border. Add additional pins before removing the quilt from the ironing board.

3. Stitch the border to the quilt with the pieced side on top (facing up). This allows you to see any triangle points and helps prevent seam allowances from flipping. A walking foot is a tremendous help when sewing borders. Press the seam allowances toward the border.

4. Measure the width of the quilt top across the middle, including the side borders just added. Cut borders to this length and sew them to the top and bottom as you did the sides.

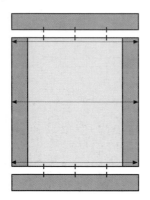

Measure center of quilt, side to side, including border strips.

5. Repeat the steps to add any additional borders.

Borders with Corner Squares

1. Lay the quilt out on a smooth surface. Measure lengthwise through the middle. Use this measurement to cut the side borders. Measure the width of the quilt through the center. Use this measurement to cut the top and bottom borders. Mark the middle and quarter points of all borders.

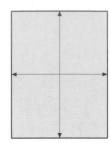

2. Position the side borders on the quilt top, right sides together, matching the ends, quarter points, and middle. Stitch the side borders to the quilt top, with the pieced side on top (facing up). Press toward the borders.

3. Sew a corner square to each end of the top and bottom border strips. Sew these to the quilt top and bottom, easing as necessary.

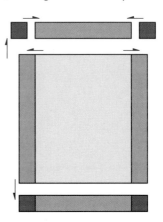

Borders with Mitered Corners

1. Measure the length and width of your quilt through the center.

2. To determine the border lengths, add twice the width of the borders plus 4" to the quilt measurements from step 1. If you are mitering multiple borders, sew all of the borders together first, pressing the seam allowances open. Use the width of the multiple borders in your calculation.

QUILTMAKING TECHNIQUES

3. Mark the centers of the borders. Use the length and width measurements from step 1 to mark the ends of the borders. Mark the quilt centers. On the wrong side of the quilt top, mark a dot ¼" in from both edges of all four corners.

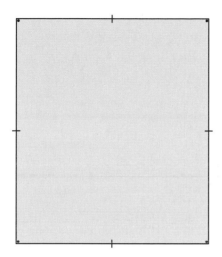

4. With right sides together, pin one border in place, matching the center and ends of the quilt and border. To join the border to the top, begin stitching one stitch out from the dot; backstitch after two or three forward stitches. Stitch forward toward the next corner. Stop one stitch before you reach the dot on the corner and backstitch. Press the seam allowances toward the border. Add the remaining borders in the same manner.

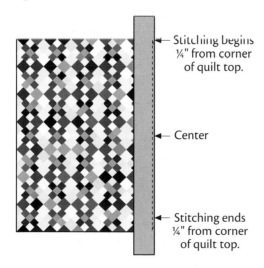

Stitching begins ¼" from corner of quilt top.

Center

Stitching ends ¼" from corner of quilt top.

5. To sew the mitered corners, first place the quilt on an ironing board. Layer the top border over the side border. Fold the top border piece at a 45° angle to the bottom piece, matching the long raw edges and

placing right sides together. If you are using multiple borders, put pins through the seams, making sure they line up. Use a square ruler with a diagonal line to check the accuracy of the fold; press.

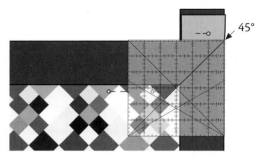

45°

Align the fold under the ruler's 45° angle.

6. Fold the two border pieces right sides together. Pin the end and edges where necessary. Draw a pencil line on the crease so you can see where to sew. Starting one stitch out from the end of the previous stitching line, stitch on the crease to the outside edge. Repeat for all four corners. Check on the right side to see that the miters are sewn correctly. Trim the excess fabric, leaving a ¼" seam allowance. Press the seam allowances open.

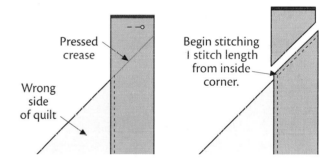

Pressed crease

Begin stitching 1 stitch length from inside corner.

Wrong side of quilt

Layering and Basting

Instructions with each project will tell you how to piece the backing. After piecing, trim the backing to 4" larger than your quilt top on all sides. The batting should also be at least 4" larger all around.

I machine quilt and use 1" safety pins to baste. If you plan to hand quilt, baste with thread in a grid about every 6". Before basting, make sure the backing and top are well pressed. I throw my batting in the clothes dryer on low heat for a few minutes to remove wrinkles.

I tape a flat button to the center of my basting table and toothpicks, at a right angle to the table edge, in the middle of each side. When placing the backing on the table, I can feel the "marks," making it easy to center the fabric. Secure the backing, right side down, to the table with masking tape or binder clips. Lay the batting out on top of the backing, smoothing out any wrinkles. Then add the quilt top and smooth out any wrinkles.

If your quilt has blocks along the outer edge, such as "The Broken Path" (page 50), make sure the corner blocks are square. If they aren't, pin them square and use steam to set them. Before pinning the center of the quilt, decide where the quilting lines will go and avoid placing pins there. If I plan to cross the middle of a block, I'll pin the edges of the block. Pin along the sides of the inner borders to keep them straight. Place pins about a fist width apart.

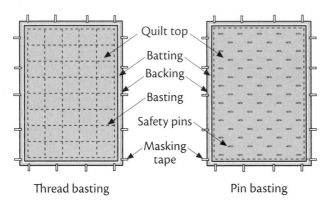

Thread basting   Pin basting

Binding

Bindings can be cut on the bias or on the straight of grain. In my experience, bias bindings wear longer and the hand sewing seems easier. Striped fabrics or plaids cut on the bias make a lovely binding. Straight-grain bindings, however, use less fabric, stretch less, and are easier to cut. Straight-grain bindings will help hold a wall hanging square.

The cutting instructions for each quilt provide the number of straight-grain strips to cut for binding. If I've used a striped fabric or a plaid cut on the bias, I've included the yardage needed for bias strips and the total number of inches needed as well. I cut my strips 2½" wide for a ⅜" finished binding. For bias strips, cut

at a 45° angle across the center of the fabric to get the longest strips possible. See "Cutting Bias Binding" (page 22) for the method I use.

1. Join the binding strips with diagonal seams. For my method refer to "Joining Binding Strips" (page 23). Press the seam allowances open. Fold the binding lengthwise, wrong sides together, and press.

2. I sew with a seam gauge and trim the quilt before attaching the binding. First stitch around the entire quilt, ⅛" from the edge of the quilt top, using a walking foot.

3. Use a large, square ruler and a long ruler to trim the quilt and make sure that the corners are square. Align the rulers with the inner border or a seam in the patchwork. If a quilt has a plain border, I trim to the edge of the fabric. If your quilt has blocks along the outer edge, such as "The Broken Path" (page 50), trim ⅛" from the edge of the blocks to allow for the ⅜" seam.

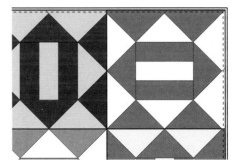

Stitch ⅛" in from the edge of the quilt top.
Trim backing and batting ⅛" beyond quilt top edge.

4. To avoid having a binding seam fall at a corner of the quilt, place the binding around the quilt using a few pins. I start on the top edge and position the binding so that the first binding seam will be sewn before I turn the upper-right corner. I continue placing the binding around the entire quilt, folding it at the quilt corners. If a binding seam hits a corner of the quilt, I reposition the entire binding. When I'm sure the binding is starting in the correct position, I remove all the pins except the one at the starting point.

5. Begin stitching 6" from the start of the binding using a ⅜" seam allowance. Bring the bobbin thread up and stitch a few inches. As you approach the first corner, stop the machine and use a small ruler to mark ⅜" from the raw edge of the corner. Sew to the mark and backstitch three stitches.

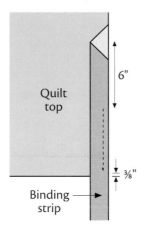

6. Remove the quilt from the machine. Fold the binding up so that it's aligned with the next edge and the fold creates a 45° angle with the corner. Turn the binding down to make a fold in the binding that is in line with the upper raw edge of the quilt top. Pin. Be absolutely sure that the fold doesn't extend beyond the quilt top. Put the quilt back under the presser foot. Lower the needle about ⅛" away from the top fold, pull up the bobbin thread, sew three stitches, backstitch three stitches, and then continue sewing until you approach the next corner. Stop ⅜" from the corner and repeat the mitering process at each corner.

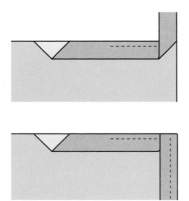

7. When stitching the last side, stop approximately 12" from the starting point. Remove the quilt from the machine. Fold the unstitched binding edges back on themselves so they just meet in the middle over the unsewn area of the quilt top. Press the folds.

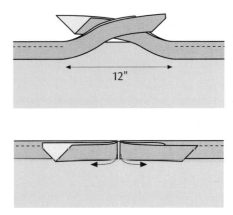

8. The easiest way to join the binding ends is to trim the ends straight across, ¼" out from the fold lines. For a diagonal seam refer to step 4 of "Joining Binding Strips" (page 23). Sew the seam. Press the seam allowance open. Repress the binding. Make certain the binding fits the unsewn area and finish sewing it to the quilt.

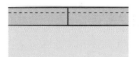

9. Turn the binding to the back of the quilt and hand sew it in place using thread that matches the binding. Miter the corners as shown.

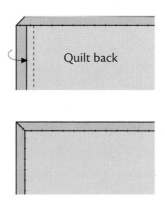

CUTTING BIAS BINDING

When I make bias binding I want as few seams as possible. For most quilts I buy 1¼ yards of fabric. This gives me a piece of fabric approximately 42" x 45", which is more or less square. Strips cut diagonally across the middle will be approximately 50" long. Some will be longer and some shorter, but I use 50" to help me determine the number of strips to cut.

1. Press the fabric. Fold on the bias to make a large triangle. The edges will not be even. If you're using a striped fabric or a plaid, make certain the lines in the fabric are at a 45° angle to the folded edge. Press the folded edge.

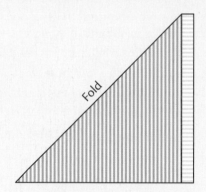

2. Gently fold the fabric a second time at a right angle to the first fold. Place the large triangle of fabric on your mat with the single fold toward you and the double fold to the left. You should be able to slide your hand between the folded layers on the left.

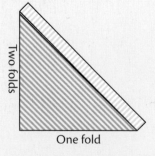

3. Place a 36"-long narrow ruler on the left edge of the fabric so that it covers both folds. Use a square ruler along the fold to align the longer ruler as shown. Remove the square ruler and trim the left edge of the fabric triangle making a straight edge.

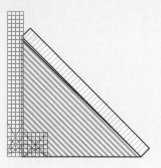

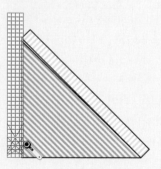

4. To cut strips, align the newly cut edge with the 2½" width on the ruler and cut. With this method you're cutting through four layers and producing two strips with each cut. Three cuts will give you six strips. If you started with 1¼ yards of fabric, you'll have approximately 300" of binding. Cut additional strips if necessary.

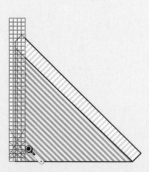

QUILTMAKING TECHNIQUES

JOINING BINDING STRIPS

1. Place a binding strip on a cutting mat. Loop the strip around so both ends are right side up. Cut the ends at the same 45° angle. Cut a ⅜" notch from one end. I consistently notch the end on my right. Repeat for all strips.

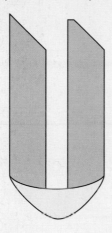

2. To join the strips, I hold the pointed end of a strip in my left hand, right side up with the point angling to the left. I place the notched end of the next strip right side down on top of the first strip, with the notch on the right.

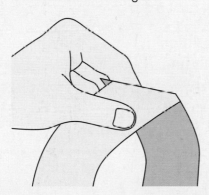

3. Pin the strips. To stitch, start at the right angle and continue through the point of the notch. This should be a ¼" seam. Leave this section under the feed dogs. Pick up the next strip and join it to the section still under the feed dogs. Continue until all strips are joined. Press the seams open. Fold the binding lengthwise wrong sides together and press.

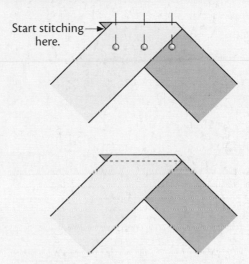

Start stitching here.

4. To join the binding ends, I like to make a diagonal seam that matches all the other binding seams. Place a dot at the intersection of the fold lines. Make a 45° cut ¼" out from the dot in the same direction as the strip end. Repeat for the other end. Sew the seam and press open. Repress the binding.

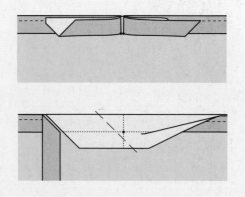

PINWHEELS revisited

Made by Lynn Roddy Brown

Finished quilt: 68" x 76" — Finished block: 6" x 6"

One of my friends found a wonderful antique pinwheel quilt at an estate sale (page 5). I don't know when I have ever been so inspired. Even though it's impossible to copy a scrap quilt exactly, especially one using fabrics that are no longer available, I made it my goal to do the very best job possible.

I kept the original quilt on a table by my design wall, examining each block in order to duplicate it. I ransacked my stash, but of course I had to shop. I often made blocks and then found a fabric I liked better, so I made more blocks. In the end I had over 40 extra blocks!

This quilt gave me permission to do all the things I hadn't done in my other quilts, such as use inconsistent values and put the same fabrics or colors next to each other. I pieced blocks that weren't pinwheels and blocks with pieced patches. I made blocks with stripes going in different directions. This was very freeing for a woman with control issues.

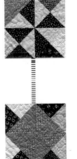

Materials

Yardage is based on 42"-wide fabric.

3⅛ yards *total* of medium/dark scraps for blocks and setting triangles

3⅛ yards *total* of light scraps for blocks and setting triangles

2¼ yards of black-and-gray print for outer borders

⅔ yard black-and-white checked fabric for binding*

5¼ yards of fabric for backing

76" x 84" piece of batting

For bias binding, you'll need 1¼ yards to make a total length of 300".

Cutting

From the medium/dark scraps for blocks, cut:
170 squares, 4¼" x 4¼" (85 matching pairs)

From the medium/dark scraps for setting triangles, cut:
12 squares, 4¼" x 4¼" (6 matching pairs)
7 squares, 6" x 6"*

From the light scraps for blocks, cut:
170 squares, 4¼" x 4¼" (85 matching pairs)

From the light scraps for setting triangles, cut:
12 squares, 4¼" x 4¼" (6 matching pairs)
7 squares, 6" x 6"*

From the *lengthwise* grain of the black-and-gray print, cut:
2 strips, 4½" x 64"
2 strips, 8½" x 72"

From the black-and-white checked fabric, cut:
8 strips, 2½" x 42"

Cut 1 square to match each pair of 4¼" squares. The seventh square can be any print.

USING STRIPES IN PINWHEEL BLOCKS

When I was making "Pinwheels Revisited," my goal was to duplicate the blocks as accurately as possible with the dark and light fabrics in the same positions and the stripes placed as they were in the original blocks. I spent a considerable amount of time trying to understand how to make the different versions of the block—the stripes can radiate out from the block center or circle around it.

Radiating out   Circling

Cutting

1. Choose one of the Pinwheel block options illustrated at right.

2. Place the striped fabric on an ironing surface right side up in the vertical or horizontal orientation indicated for the selected option. Be certain both squares are positioned in the same way. Pair medium/dark and light fabric squares as described in "Paired Fabrics" (page 10).

OR

3. Make the diagonal cuts from the lower-right corner to the upper-left corner; be certain to keep the squares (and stripes) in the same position as step 2.

Block Options

Option 1: Place the light stripe on the bottom, right side up and going vertically.

Option 2: Place the light stripe on the bottom, right side up and going horizontally.

Option 3: Place the dark stripe on the bottom, right side up and going vertically.

Option 4: Place the dark stripe on the bottom, right side up and going horizontally.

Making the Pinwheel Blocks

1. Follow the cutting guidelines for your chosen block option, and refer to "Making Two Identical Half-Square-Triangle Units" (page 11).

2. Arrange the four matching half-square-triangle units according to your block illustration. Sew the units together in rows; press the seam allowances open. Join the rows: press the seam allowances open.

Pinwheel Blocks

The quilt has about 59 of Pinwheel block A, about 25 of block B, and one of block C for a total of 85 blocks. The difference between the blocks is simply the value placement. Scattered randomly across the quilt surface, these blocks will create alternate patterns. Most of the blocks use two fabrics. A few odd blocks, such as block C, use additional fabrics and are made with half-square-triangle units arranged in other patterns. The instructions are written for two fabrics with the values positioned as shown in block A. Reverse the values in your blocks to create as many of block B as you like, and throw in a block C if desired. It's up to you to decide how scrappy you want your quilt. Note that in blocks A and B, the half-square-triangle units are simply positioned in different ways when sewn together. This opposite placement of the half-square-triangle units creates pinwheels that turn in opposite directions.

Block A   Block B

Block C

For each block you'll need two matching (or not) medium/dark 4¼" squares and two matching light 4¼" squares.

1. Pair each pair of light squares with a pair of medium/dark squares. Referring to "Making Two Identical Half-Square-Triangle Units" (page 11), make two identical pieced squares from each.

Press the seam allowances toward the medium/dark fabric and trim the units to 3½" square. Make 85 matching sets of four.

Make 85 sets of four.

2. Arrange four matching units as shown. Make certain the light and medium/dark fabrics are in the correct positions. Sew the units together in rows; press the seam allowances open. Join the rows: press the seam allowances open. Feel free to make a few blocks with unmatched units or blocks with the units in odd positions. Make a total of 85 blocks.

Make 85.

Making Pieced Setting Triangles

In the original antique quilt, some of the setting triangles were pieced as one half of a Pinwheel block. These were probably extra blocks that were cut in half. For many of the pieced triangles, there seemed to be no thought given to value or pattern. Maybe the quiltmaker was just using up odd scraps. The instructions are written for the most efficient use of fabric—half Pinwheel blocks made in sets of four. This will give you three sets of four identical triangles as shown in triangle A. Feel free to vary them as the original quiltmaker did, shown in triangles B, C, and D.

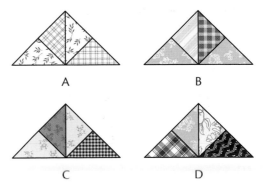

A   B

C   D

For each set of four setting triangles, you'll need:

- Two matching 4¼" squares and one 6" square of the same medium/dark fabric

- Two matching 4¼" squares and one 6" square of the same light fabric

1. Pair each of the medium/dark 4¼" squares with a light 4¼" square. Referring to "Making Two Identical Half-Square-Triangle Units" (page 11), make two identical pieced squares from each. Press the seam allowances toward the medium/dark fabric and trim the units to 3½" square.

Make 4.

2. Cut both of the 6" squares into quarters diagonally to yield eight quarter-square triangles. Using a half-square-triangle unit from step 1, one light quarter-square triangle, and one medium/dark quarter-square triangle, arrange the units as shown below. Note that the quarter-square triangles are slightly oversized.

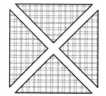

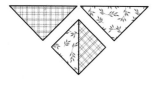

3. Matching the corners, sew a medium/dark triangle to the half-square-triangle unit. Press toward the triangle. Trim the point. Add the light triangle as shown. Press outward. Make four.

Trim.

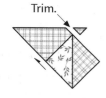
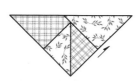

Make 4.

4. Repeat steps 1–3 until you have made a total of 24 side setting triangles.

Making Pieced Corner Triangles

For four corner triangles using the same fabrics: Pair a light 6" square with a medium/dark 6" square. Referring to "Making Two Identical Half-Square-Triangle Units" (page 11), make two identical pieced squares. Press the seam allowances open. Don't trim the units. Cut the units in half diagonally, across the seam.

For four corner triangles using different fabrics: Join odd quarter-square triangles cut from 6" squares as shown below. Press the seams open.

Assembling the Quilt Top

1. Referring to the quilt diagram, arrange the blocks, pieced setting triangles, and pieced corner triangles in a diagonal set on a design wall. Arrange the blocks in a way that you find pleasing. When identical fabrics or similar values touch, alternate patterns will form. The more this happens, the scrappier the quilt.

2. Referring to "Diagonal Sets" (page 16), sew the pieced side setting triangles and blocks together

into diagonal rows. Press the seam allowances open. Join the rows and press the seam allowances open. Add the corner triangles; press the seam allowances outward.

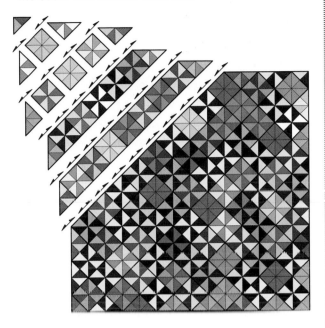

3. Trim the quilt on all four sides, leaving a ¼" seam allowance.

4. Refer to "Borders with Butted Corners" (page 17). Using the 4½" x 64" strips, add the side gray-and-black print outer borders. For the top and bottom borders, use the 8½" x 72" strips.

Finishing the Quilt

1. Cut the backing fabric, across the grain, into two equal pieces. Remove the selvages. Sew these pieces together along the lengthwise grain to create the quilt back. Press the seams open. The seam will run vertically on the quilt.

2. Layer and baste the quilt (page 19).

3. Hand or machine quilt as desired.

4. Refer to "Binding" (page 20) to use the black-and-white checked 2½"-wide strips to bind the quilt.

5. Make and attach a label to your quilt.

"Antique Pinwheels" owned by Nona Hoecker. Machine quilted by Jane Plisga; finished by Lynn Roddy Brown. This is the original quilt that inspired Lynn to make "Pinwheels Revisited."

LYNN SAYS:
NEW PROJECT—NO PROBLEM!

I often hear quilters lament that they can't possibly start a new project, because they have too many UFOs (unfinished objects). My reply is this: "If you already own the fabric, why not?"

LEFTovers

Made by Lynn Roddy Brown
Finished quilt: 53" x 61½" — Finished block: 6" x 6"

After making "Pinwheels Revisited" (page 24), I had more than 40 extra blocks. I challenged myself to create a second quilt without making additional blocks. "Leftovers" uses 32 of those leftover blocks.

The value placement in the blocks creates pinwheels that appear to spin in opposite directions. In "Pinwheels Revisited," the two blocks were placed randomly. In this quilt, the blocks with opposite values were placed in alternate rows. This helps create a more consistent secondary pattern of larger pinwheels. Inconsistent values within the blocks may blur the pattern in some places. If all the blocks used very light and dark values, you would have a clear secondary pattern, but the quilt might not be as interesting.

Materials

Yardage is based on 42"-wide fabric.

1⅛ yards *total* of medium/dark scraps for blocks*

1⅛ yards *total* of light scraps for blocks*

1⅓ yards of blue-and-white print for setting triangles and pieced border

⅞ yard of red print for pieced border and corner blocks

1¾ yards of brown print for outer border

⅝ yard of navy print for binding

3¾ yards of fabric for backing

61" x 70" piece of batting

**64 squares, 5 " x 5", in matching pairs are an option.*

Cutting

From the medium/dark scraps, cut:
64 squares, 4¼" x 4¼" (32 matching pairs)

From the light scraps, cut:
64 squares, 4¼" x 4¼" (32 matching pairs)

From the blue-and-white print, cut:
4 squares, 11" x 11"; cut each square into quarters diagonally to yield 16 side triangles (2 are extra)

2 squares, 6½" x 6½"; cut each square in half diagonally to yield 4 corner triangles

5 squares, 9¾" x 9¾ "; cut each square into quarters diagonally to yield 20 border triangles (2 are extra)

From the red print, cut:
2 strips, 9¾" x 42"; crosscut into 6 squares, 9¾" x 9¾". Cut 4 of the squares into quarters diagonally to yield 16 border triangles (2 are extra). Cut 2 of the squares in half diagonally to yield 4 corner triangles.

4 squares, 5½" x 5½", for corner squares

From the brown print, cut:
4 strips, 5½" x 56", from the *lengthwise* grain

From the navy print, cut:
7 strips, 2½" x 42"

Making the Blocks

This quilt uses the two blocks shown below. The difference between the blocks is the placement of the values. For each block you'll need two matching medium/dark 4¼" squares and two matching light 4¼" squares.

Block A   Block B

1. Pair each pair of light squares with a pair of medium/dark squares. Referring to "Making Two Identical Half-Square-Triangle Units" (page 11), make two identical pieced squares from each. Press the seam allowances toward the medium/ dark fabric and trim the units to 3½" square. Make 32 matching sets of four.

2. Lay out the units as shown for block A. Make certain the light and medium/dark fabrics are in the correct positions. Sew the units together in rows; press the seam allowances open. Join the rows and press the seam allowances open. Make 20 blocks.

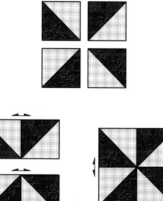

Make 20.

3. Lay out the units as shown for block B, making certain the light and medium/dark fabrics are in the correct positions. Sew the units together in rows; press the seam allowances open. Join the rows and press the seam allowances open. Make 12 blocks.

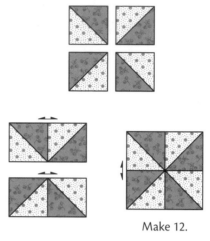

Make 12.

Assembling the Quilt Top

1. Working on a design wall and referring to the quilt diagram, arrange blocks A and B in diagonal rows on a design wall. Blocks A and B alternate in the diagonal rows. All rows start and end with block A.

2. Add the blue-and-white print side triangles to the layout. Referring to "Diagonal Sets" (page 16), join the blocks and side triangles in diagonal rows. Press the seam allowances open. Add the corner triangles; press the seam allowances outward.

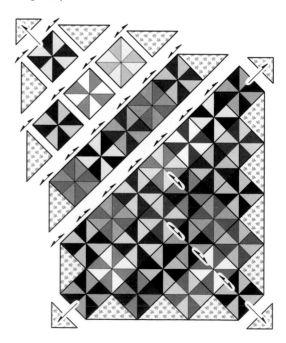

3. Trim the quilt on all four sides, leaving a ¼" seam allowance beyond the block points.

4. Sewing the triangles for the pieced border is much easier if the triangle points are trimmed. To trim the points, you can use a special point-trimmer ruler or a rotary ruler with ⅛" marks. Align the ⅜" line with a short edge of the triangle. Position the ruler so the corner is just touching the long edge of the triangle as shown. Trim the point. Rotate the triangle and trim the second point. Repeat for all 18 blue-and-white triangles and 14 red print triangles.

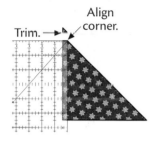

Align corner.
Trim.

5. Each pieced border starts and ends with a blue-and-white triangle. To join the border triangles, place a blue-and-white triangle right sides together with a red print triangle as shown. Notice the position of the ¼" seam line in relation to the trimmed point. Sew the seam and press open. Join four blue-and-white triangles and three red print triangles for both the top and bottom borders. Piece the side borders in the same manner using five blue-and-white triangles and four red print triangles each.

Top/bottom border.
Make 2.

Side border.
Make 2.

6. Add the side borders using pins and a steam iron if necessary to adjust the fit. Press the seam allowances open. Add the top and bottom borders. Press the seam allowances open. Add the corner triangles and press outward. Trim the corner triangles.

7. Referring to "Borders with Corner Squares" (page 18), add the outer borders using the brown print border strips and red print corner squares.

Finishing the Quilt

1. Cut the backing fabric across the grain into two equal pieces. Remove the selvages. Sew these pieces together along the lengthwise grain to create the quilt back. Press the seams open. The seam will run vertically on the quilt.

2. Layer and baste the quilt (page 19).

3. Hand or machine quilt as desired.

4. Refer to "Binding" (page 20) to use the navy print 2½"-wide strips to bind the quilt.

5. Make and attach a label to your quilt.

broken dishes MEDALLION

Made by Lynn Roddy Brown
Finished quilt: 78½" x 78½" — Finished block: 6" x 6"

I had a stash of half-square-triangle units that came from a block swap, and I put them to good use in this quilt. Participating in a block swap is an easy way to get a wide variety of colors and prints for a very scrappy quilt. When making this quilt, I applied my "do the next right thing" rule, beginning with the center of the quilt. I couldn't decide on additional border fabrics until after I sewed together the center with the gold striped border. When I put the center section on my design wall, it was much easier to audition fabrics for the next border. I made decisions as I worked outward and did what seemed right for the quilt at the time.

Because this is a medallion quilt with pieced borders as well as unpieced borders, accuracy is very important. The center needs to be the correct measurement for each subsequent pieced border to fit properly.

Materials

Yardage is based on 42"-wide fabric.

2½ yards *total* of medium/dark scraps for blocks*

2½ yards *total* of light scraps for blocks*

½ yard of gold striped fabric for inner border**

1⅓ yards light green print for second border

2⅛ yards of red print 1 for outer border

¾ yard of red print 2 for binding

7½ yards of fabric for backing

87" x 87" piece of batting

170 squares, 5" x 5", in matching pairs are another option.

**If your stripe happens to run crosswise, you'll need ⅝ yard.*

Cutting

From the medium/dark scraps, cut:
170 squares, 4¼" x 4¼" (85 matching pairs)

From the light scraps, cut:
170 squares, 4¼" x 4¼" (85 matching pairs)

From the gold striped fabric, cut:
2 strips, 6½" x 42"; crosscut into 4 strips, 6½" x 21"*

From the light green print, cut:
4 strips, 6½" x 44", from the *lengthwise* grain

From red print 1, cut:
4 strips, 6½" x 70", from the *lengthwise* grain

From red print 2, cut:
9 strips, 2½" x 42"

The stripe I used ran parallel to the selvage. If your stripe runs crossgrain, cut 4 lengthwise strips, 6½" x 21".

Making the Blocks

For each block you'll need two matching medium/dark 4¼" squares and two matching light 4¼" squares.

1. Pair each pair of light squares with a pair of medium/dark squares. Referring to "Making Two Identical Half-Square-Triangle Units" (page 11), make two identical pieced squares from each. Press the seam allowances toward the medium/dark fabric and trim the units to 3½" square.

2. Lay out the units as shown. Make certain the light and medium/dark fabrics are in the correct positions. Sew the units together in rows; press the seam allowances open. Join the rows: press the seam allowances open.

3. Repeat steps 1 and 2 to make a total of 85 blocks. The Broken Dishes blocks should measure 6½" x 6½".

Assembling the Quilt Top

1. Arrange nine Broken Dishes blocks in three horizontal rows of three blocks each, referring to the quilt diagram on the facing page. Make certain the blocks are all positioned with a dark triangle in the upper-left corner. Join the blocks in rows. Press the seam allowances open. Join the rows. Press the seam allowances open. This center unit should measure 18½" x 18½". If you get a different measurement, check your seam allowances and make adjustments as necessary.

2. Referring to "Borders with Corner Squares" (page 18), add the gold striped borders using four Broken Dishes blocks in the corners. Be certain the blocks are positioned as shown in the quilt diagram.

3. Arrange and sew five Broken Dishes blocks together as shown to make a side border row. Press the seams open. Arrange and sew seven Broken Dishes blocks together as shown to make a top or bottom border row; press the seams open. Make two of each.

Make 2.

Make 2.

4. Sew the five-block border rows from step 3 to the side edges of the quilt top. Press the seams open. Sew the seven-block border rows to the top and bottom edges of the quilt top. Press the seams open. The top should measure 42½" x 42½".

5. Referring to "Borders with Corner Squares" (page 18), add the light green print borders using four Broken Dishes blocks in the corners. Be certain the blocks are positioned as shown in the quilt diagram.

6. Arrange and sew nine Broken Dishes blocks together as shown to make a side border row. Press the seams open. Arrange and sew eleven Broken Dishes blocks together as shown to make a top or bottom border row; press the seams open. Make two of each.

Make 2.

Make 2.

7. Sew the nine-block border rows from step 8 to the side edges of the quilt top. Press the seams open. Sew the eleven-block border rows to the top and bottom edges of the quilt top. Press the seams open. The top should measure 66½" x 66½".

8. Referring to "Borders with Corner Squares" (page 18), add the red print 1 outer borders using four Broken Dishes blocks in the corners. Be certain the blocks are positioned as shown in the quilt diagram.

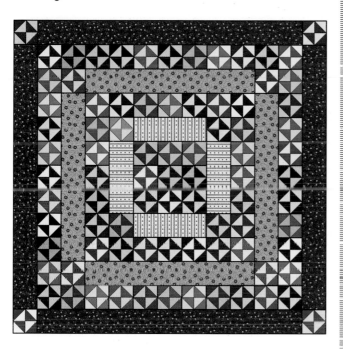

Finishing the Quilt

1. Cut the backing fabric across the grain into three equal pieces. Remove the selvages. Sew these pieces together along the lengthwise grain to create the quilt back. Press the seams open. The seams can run vertically or horizontally.

2. Layer and baste the quilt (page 19).

3. Hand or machine quilt as desired.

4. Refer to "Binding" (page 20) to use the 2½"-wide red print 2 strips to bind the quilt.

5. Make and attach a label to your quilt.

zigzag CEDARS

Made by Lynn Roddy Brown
Finished quilt: 61½" x 68½" — Finished block: 12" x 12"

I love having a stockpile of half-square-triangle units. As with "Broken Dishes Medallion" (page 34), the units in this quilt came from a block swap. When sorting through them, I chose a wide variety of colors and prints for a very scrappy quilt. Groups of four different units were joined to make the Little Cedar Tree blocks. These were sewn together in groups of four to make the larger blocks. The black-and-white background fabric was in my stash; it was one of three fabrics I bought as a possible border for "Pinwheels Revisited" (page 24). I found the red border fabric on a sale shelf and bought it to have as a quilt backing. The binding was made for another quilt but was not used when a better option appeared. I consider any quilt that comes entirely from my stash as free—this is a free quilt!

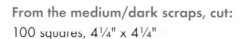

Materials

Yardage is based on 42"-wide fabric.

2⅛ yards of black-and-white print for setting triangles

2⅛ yards of red-and-black print for side borders

1⅝ yards *total* of medium/dark scraps for blocks*

1⅝ yards *total* of light scraps for blocks*

1 yard of burgundy striped fabric for bias binding**

4¼ yards of fabric for backing

70" x 77" piece of batting

*100 charm squares, 5 " x 5", are an option.

**If you cut crossgrain binding strips, ⅝ yard is enough

Cutting

From the medium/dark scraps, cut:
100 squares, 4¼" x 4¼"

From the light scraps, cut:
100 squares, 4¼" x 4¼"

From the black-and-white print, cut:
3 strips, 19½" x 42"; crosscut into 5 squares, 19½" x 19½". Cut each square into quarters diagonally to yield 20 side triangles.

4 squares, 10½" x 10½"; cut each square in half diagonally to yield 8 corner triangles

From the red-and-black print, cut from the *lengthwise* grain:
2 strips, 5½" x 72"

From the burgundy striped fabric, cut:
2½"-wide bias strips to total 272" (or 7 crossgrain strips, 2½" x 42")

Making the Blocks

For this quilt, you'll need 11 full blocks and two partial blocks. Each full block is made from four cedar-tree units. Partial blocks are made from three cedar-tree units.

1. Referring to "Making Two Identical Half-Square-Triangle Units" (page 11), pair a light 4¼" square with a medium/dark 4¼" square. Make two identical half-square-triangle units from each pair for a total of 200. Press the seam allowances toward the medium/dark fabric and trim the units to 3½" square.

2. Select four different half-square-triangle units. Arrange the units as shown. Sew the units together in rows and press the seam allowances open. Sew the rows together and press the seam allowances open. Make 50 cedar-tree units.

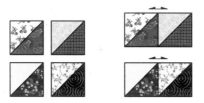

Make 50.

3. Select four different cedar-tree units. Arrange the units as shown. Make certain the light corner of two units and the dark corner of two units form the block center. Sew the units in rows and press the seam allowances open. Sew the rows together

and press the seam allowances open. Make 11 Little Cedar Tree blocks.

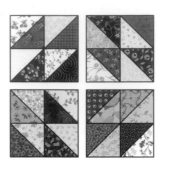

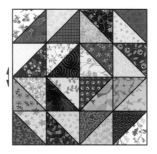

Make 11.

4. For the partial blocks, select three cedar-tree units. Arrange the units as shown. Make certain the center values alternate. Sew the upper units into a row and press the seam allowances open. Join the lower unit and press toward the lower unit. Make two partial blocks.

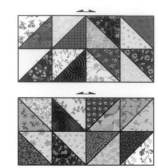

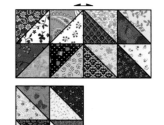

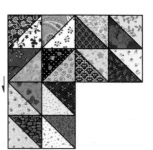

Make 2.

Assembling the Quilt Top

1. Arrange the full blocks, partial blocks, side triangles, and corner triangles into three vertical panels as shown. Panels 1 and 3 each have four full blocks, six side triangles, and four corner triangles. The center panel has three full blocks, two partial blocks, and eight side triangles. Referring to "Diagonal Sets" (page 16), align the corners of the triangles with the corners of the blocks and sew together. Press the seam allowances toward the triangles. Trim the triangle points even with the edge of the blocks.

2. Join the units into panels, aligning the seams. Add the corner triangles to panels 1 and 3 and press the seam allowances outward.

3. Trim each panel on the two long sides, leaving a ¼" seam allowance beyond the block points.

4. Join the panels and press the seam allowances open.

5. Mark the cutting line on the partial blocks at the top and bottom of panel 2 so that it's ¼" away from the centers of the cedar-tree units. Stitch just inside this line to stabilize the edge; when trimmed, the edges will be on the bias. Trim the top and bottom of the quilt top, leaving a ¼" seam allowance beyond the tips of the blocks in panels 1 and 3 and cutting along the marked line in panel 2.

6. Referring to "Borders with Butted Corners" (page 17), add the red-and-black print side borders using the 5½" x 72" strips. Press the seam allowances toward the borders.

Finishing the Quilt

1. Cut the backing fabric across the grain into two equal pieces. Remove the selvages. Sew these pieces together along the lengthwise grain to create the quilt back. Press the seam open. The seam will run crosswise on the quilt.

2. Layer and baste the quilt (page 19).

3. Hand or machine quilt as desired.

4. Refer to "Binding" (page 20) to use the burgundy striped 2½"-wide strips to bind the quilt.

5. Make and attach a label to your quilt.

RADIANT REDS

Made by Elizabeth (Liz) Broussard
Finished quilt: 62½" x 62½" — Finished block: 6" x 6"

My friend Liz loves batiks. Here she used a fabulous dark blue batik along with 16 different red, pink, and orange beauties. The quilt is designed to use fat eighths, which are approximately 9" x 21". This is a perfect opportunity to use a collection you have been saving for a special project. Liz wanted to make a quilt entirely of half-square-triangle units. Sashing strips between each four-unit block make the assembly easy, avoiding the problem of matching a lot of seam intersections. Because Liz doesn't like to miter binding corners, her solution was to round off the corners. The soft corners add a welcome touch to what is otherwise a striking, but very angular design.

Materials

Yardage is based on 42"-wide fabric.

4⅛ yards of navy batik for blocks, sashing, sashing squares, and borders

1 fat eighth *each* of 16 different red, pink, and orange batiks

⅝ yard of pink batik for binding*

4⅓ yards for backing

71" x 71" piece of batting

For bias binding (recommended for rounded corners), you'll need 1 yard to make a total length of 262".

Cutting

From the navy batik, cut:
8 strips, 8½" x 42"; crosscut into 32 squares, 8½" x 8½"

26 strips, 1½" x 42"; crosscut into:*

    32 strips, 1½" x 6½"

    32 strips, 1½" x 13½"

    4 strips, 1½" x 27½"

    5 squares, 1½" x 1½"

7 strips, 4" x 42"

From *each* of the fat eighths, cut:
2 squares, 8½" x 8½" (32 total)

From the pink batik, cut:
7 strips, 2½" x 42"

If your fabric is a full 42" wide after washing and removing selvages, 21 strips may be enough.

Making the Blocks

You'll make four identical blocks from *each* of the 16 fat eighths.

1. Select two matching red, pink, or orange 8½" squares. Pair these squares with two navy 8½" squares. Refer to "Making Eight Identical Half-Square-Triangle Units" (page 11) to make a total of 16 identical units. Press the seam allowances toward the navy and trim the units to 3½" square.

Make 16.

2. Arrange four of the half-square-triangle units from step 1 as shown. Sew the units together in rows. Press the seam allowances open. Sew the rows together, carefully matching the seams. Press the final seam allowances open. Make four blocks.

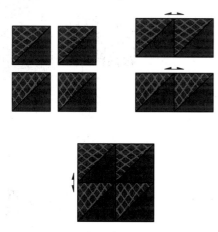

Make 4.

3. Repeat steps 1 and 2 to make a total of 64 blocks.

Assembling the Quilt Top

The directions are written so that you construct the quilt in four quadrants. I feel that this will give you the best chance of getting all of the blocks in the correct positions and having a square quilt. The blocks were made in sets of four. One block will be used in each quadrant of the quilt. The sashing includes sashing squares made of the same fabric. This helps to keep the blocks aligned and makes it easier to keep the quilt square.

1. On a design wall, place one block from each set to make a quadrant, rotating the blocks as shown. Arrange the blocks until you find the color placement pleasing.

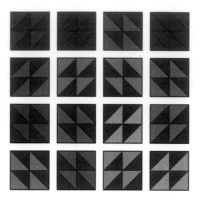

2. Assign a number to each of the 16 blocks in the quadrant as indicated. Pin a piece of paper to each block.

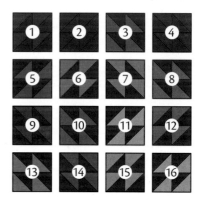

3. Starting with the four blocks in the upper-left corner, assign a letter to each block and write it on your piece of paper (1A, 2B, 5C, 6D). Remove these four blocks from the wall and arrange them with two 1½" x 6½" sashing strips and one 1½" x 13½" sashing strip as shown. You'll essentially be dividing your quadrant up into four smaller quadrants to sew them together.

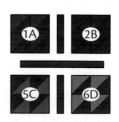

4. Sew the horizontal rows of blocks and sashing strips together. Press toward the sashing. Sew the rows to each side of the 1½" x 13½" sashing strip. Press toward the sashing. Return the unit to the design wall keeping it in the correct position.

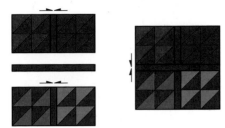

5. Repeat steps 3 and 4 to make four large units.

6. Remove the four large units from the design wall and arrange them with four 1½" x 13½" sashing strips and one 1½" sashing square as shown.

7. Sew the horizontal rows of units and sashing strips together. Press toward the sashing. Join the horizontal row of sashing strips and sashing square. Press toward the sashing. Join the rows. Press toward the sashing. This completes the upper-left quadrant. Return it to the design wall.

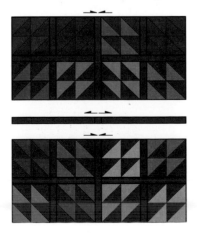

8. Use the placement chart to arrange the remaining quadrants and repeat steps 3–7 for each. The upper-left and lower-right quadrants are the same; the upper-right and lower-left quadrants are the same.

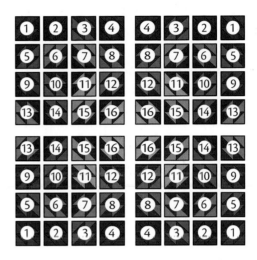

9. Arrange the quadrants, four 1½" x 27½" sashing strips, and one 1½" sashing square as shown. Sew the upper quadrants and sashing strip together, and then sew the lower quadrants and sashing strip together. Press the seam allowances toward the sashing. Join the horizontal row of sashing strips and sashing square. Press toward the sashing strip. Join the top and bottom quadrants together with the sashing row. Press toward the sashing.

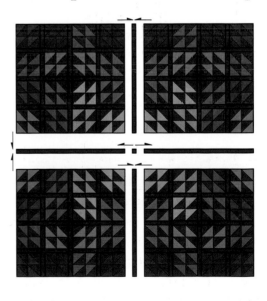

10. For each of the side borders, sew two 4" x 42" navy strips end to end using a diagonal seam. Press the seam allowances open. Refer to "Borders with Butted Corners" (page 17) to add the side borders. Press the seam allowances toward the border.

11. For the top and bottom borders, cut one 4" x 42" navy strip into two equal lengths. Sew a half strip to each of two 4" x 42" strips using a diagonal seam. Press the seam allowances open. Add the top and bottom borders. Press the seam allowances toward the border.

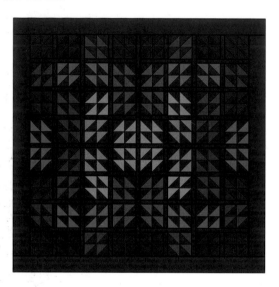

Finishing the Quilt

1. Cut the backing fabric across the grain into two equal pieces. Remove the selvages. Sew these pieces together along the lengthwise grain to create the quilt back. Press the seam open. The seam will run vertically or horizontally on the quilt.

2. Layer and baste the quilt (page 19).

3. Hand or machine quilt as desired.

4. If you would like to create the rounded corners, refer to "Rounded Corners" (at right) before adding the binding. Refer to "Binding" (page 20) and use the pink 2½"-wide strips to bind the quilt.

5. Make and attach a label to your quilt.

ROUNDED CORNERS

1. Use a saucer or other round edge for your pattern. Mark the curve on the quilt top. (I like Ivory soap slivers for marking; Liz's choice is a rolling chalk marker.)

Mark curve.

2. Using a walking foot and starting in the middle of a side, stitch around the entire quilt, ⅛" from the edge of the quilt top. When you reach the corners, stitch ⅛" inside the marked curve. Trim the corners ⅛" outside the stitching line.

3. Refer to "Cutting Bias Binding Strips" (page 22). Make one long binding strip that's at least 262" long.

4. Starting in the middle of a side, attach the binding with a walking foot. As you stitch around the corners, I suggest that you stitch slowly and stop often, lowering the needle, raising the presser foot, and readjusting the binding as needed.

SHATTERED DISHES

Made by Lynn Roddy Brown

Finished quilt: 57½" x 69½" – Finished block: 8½" x 8½"

In this quilt, I used Civil War reproduction prints and shirtings, which are very light prints used for men's shirts in the mid- to late-nineteenth century. Using these "related" fabrics is an easy way for a beginning scrap quilter to make a pleasing quilt. The reproduction prints give a very old-fashioned look to your quilt. This quilt would lend itself to other types of fabrics as well, from '30s reproduction prints to bright contemporary prints. But don't be afraid to mix and match fabrics as well. Remember, it's the contrast in value that's most important.

Materials

Yardage is based on 42"-wide fabric.

1 fat eighth *each of* 32 medium/dark prints for blocks*

1 fat eighth *each of* 32 light prints for blocks*

2 yards of blue striped fabric for outer borders

1 yard of purple print for setting triangles

⅝ yard of burgundy fabric for binding

4 yards of fabric for backing

66" x 78" piece of batting

*If you use scraps, you'll need pieces that are approximately 9" x 11".

Cutting

From *each* of the medium/dark prints, cut:
2 squares, 4¼" x 4¼" (64 total)
1 square, 6" x 6" (32 total)

From *each* of the light prints, cut:
2 squares, 4¼" x 4¼" (64 total)
1 square, 6" x 6" (32 total)

From the purple print, cut:
4 squares, 14¼" x 14¼"; cut each square into quarters diagonally to yield 16 side triangles (2 are extra)
2 squares, 8" x 8"; cut each square in half diagonally to yield 4 corner triangles

From the blue striped fabric, cut:
4 strips, 5" x 64", from the *lengthwise* grain*

From the burgundy fabric, cut:
7 strips, 2½" x 42"

*If you're using striped fabric for the border, refer to "Fussy Cutting Stripes" (page 17).

Making the Blocks

The instructions are written for making one block at a time. For each block, you'll need:

- 2 squares, 4¼" x 4¼", and 1 square, 6" x 6", from the same medium/dark fabric

- 2 squares, 4¼" x 4¼", and 1 square, 6" x 6", from the same light fabric

1. Pair each light 4¼" square with a medium/dark 4¼" square. Referring to "Making Two Identical Half-Square-Triangle Units" (page 11), make two identical pieced squares from each. Press the seam allowances toward the medium/dark fabric and trim the units to 3½" square.

2. Lay out the units as shown. Make certain the light and medium/dark fabrics are in the correct positions. Sew the units together in rows; press the seam allowances open. Join the rows: press the seam allowances open.

3. Pair the medium/dark 6" square with the light 6" square. Referring to "Making Two Identical Half-Square-Triangle Units" (page 11), make two identical pieced squares. Press the seam allowances open. Do not trim. Cut each half-square-triangle unit in half diagonally across the seam to create four quarter-square units. These units are slightly oversized and will be trimmed in the next step.

Make 2.

4. Arrange the quarter-square units around the unit from step 2 as shown. Match the seams and sew the quarter-square units to the center unit, referring to "Square-in-a-Square Units" (page 15). Press away from the center. Trim the block to 9" x 9".

5. Repeat steps 1–4 to make 32 blocks.

Assembling the Quilt Top

1. Working on a design wall and referring to the quilt diagram, arrange the Shattered Dishes blocks and the side setting triangles into diagonal rows.

2. Sew the blocks and side setting triangles into diagonal rows, referring to "Diagonal Sets" (page 16). Press the seam allowances open.

3. Join the rows and press the seam allowances open. Add the corner triangles; press the seam allowances outward.

4. Trim the quilt on all four sides, leaving a ¼" seam allowance beyond the block points.

5. Referring to "Borders with Butted Corners" (page 17), add the side borders and then the top and bottom borders.

Finishing the Quilt

1. Cut the backing fabric across the grain into two equal pieces. Remove the selvages. Sew these pieces together along the lengthwise grain to create the quilt back. Press the seams open. The seam will run horizontally on the quilt.

2. Layer and baste the quilt (page 19).

3. Hand or machine quilt as desired.

4. Refering to "Binding" (page 20), use the burgundy 2½"-wide strips to bind the quilt.

5. Make and attach a label to your quilt.

the BROKEN PATH

Made by Lynn Roddy Brown
Finished quilt: 63½" x 72½" — Finished block: 9" x 9"

I saw a tiny picture of an antique quilt using the Broken Path block and instantly knew I had to make one. I used fabrics in this quilt that have been in my stash for years. These fabrics had extreme visual textures or strange colors that I felt matched nothing else. Usually when I'm making a quilt, I make about two thirds of the blocks I think I will need and put them on the design wall. Then I make a cup of tea, sit in my chair, and decide which blocks I will use and what blocks I still need to make to finish the quilt. With this quilt it didn't seem to matter what I added. It all looked good to me. I was amazed. I think there's a level of busyness that once you cross over, it doesn't matter what you use. This is another free quilt—all materials came from my stash.

Materials

Yardage is based on 42"-wide fabric.

4¼ yards *total* of medium/dark scraps for blocks

3⅝ yards *total* of light scraps for blocks

⅔ yard of brown-and-gold plaid for binding*

4⅛ yards of fabric for backing**

72" x 81" piece of batting

*For bias binding, you'll need 1 yard to make a total length of 284".

**This yardage uses a horizontal seam and allows 3 extra inches at the top and bottom instead of the usual 4. For a vertical seam you'll need 5 yards.

Cutting

For 1 Block (Cut 56 Total.)

From one medium/dark scrap, cut:
2 rectangles, 2" x 5½"
1 square, 5" x 5"
1 square, 6½" x 6½"

From one light scrap, cut:
1 rectangle, 2" x 5½"
1 square, 5" x 5"
1 square, 6½" x 6½"

For Binding

From the brown-and-gold plaid, cut:
8 strips, 2½" x 42"

Making the Blocks

1. Sew matching medium/dark rectangles to each side of a light rectangle. Press the seam allowances toward the medium/dark fabric. Trim and square up the left edge; cut a 5"-wide segment. Measure the square and make certain that it's 5" x 5".

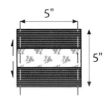

2. Use spray starch to press each of the 5" squares; cut them in half diagonally. Placing the unit from step 1 in the center, arrange the triangles as shown. Referring to "Square-in-a-Square Units" (page 15), add the triangles to the center square. Press the seam allowances away from the center. Trim the block ¼" beyond the points of the rail unit so that it measures 6⅞" x 6⅞".

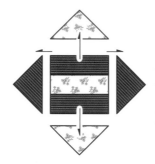

3. Pair the medium/dark 6½" square with the light 6½" square. Referring to "Making Two Identical Half-Square-Triangle Units" (page 11), make two identical pieced squares. Press the seam allowances open. Cut each half-square-triangle unit in half diagonally across the seam to create four quarter-square units.

Make 2.

4. Place a quarter-square unit on each side of the unit from step 2. Sew the quarter-square units to the center unit, referring to "Square-in-a-Square Units" (page 15). Press away from the center. Trim the block ¼" beyond the points of the center pieced square so that the block measures 9½" x 9½".

5. Repeat steps 1–4 to make 56 blocks.

Assembling the Quilt Top

1. Arrange the Broken Path blocks in eight horizontal rows of seven blocks each on a design wall, rotating the blocks as shown in the quilt diagram.

2. Sew the blocks into rows; press the seam allowances open. Join the rows and press the seam allowances open.

Finishing the Quilt

1. Cut the backing fabric across the grain into two equal pieces. Remove the selvages. Sew these pieces together along the lengthwise grain to create the quilt back. Press the seams open. The seam will run horizontally on the quilt.

2. Layer and baste the quilt (page 19).

3. Hand or machine quilt as desired.

4. Refer to "Binding" (page 20) to use the brown-and-gold plaid 2½"-wide strips to bind the quilt.

5. Make and attach a label to your quilt.

TEXAS windmills

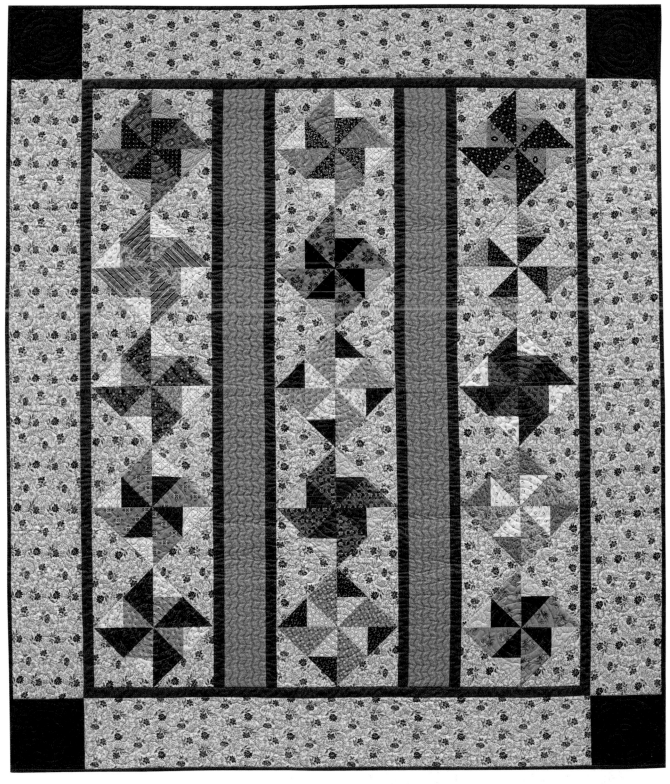

Made by Lynn Roddy Brown

Finished quilt: 63" x 73" — Finished block: 8" x 8"

Windmill blocks create strong, distinct patterns when they're made using three contrasting values. I like to choose a very dark print, usually a tone-on-tone; a medium print; and a light fabric. When you look at the blocks in this quilt, you'll see the values placed in different positions. The varying placement of light, medium, and dark has a dramatic impact on the look of the block. To the untrained eye, they may even appear to be different blocks. Many antique quilts use the same block but with varied value placement. Studying antique quilts is a good way to develop your own approach to making scrap quilts.

Materials

Yardage is based on 42"-wide fabric.

3⅛ yards of purple-and-white print for setting triangles and borders

1⅝ yards *total* of light, medium, and dark scraps for blocks

1⅞ yards of light green print for vertical strips

⅝ yard of dark green print for vertical sashing and inner border

⅞ yard of dark purple fabric for corner squares and binding

5 yards of fabric for backing

71" x 81" piece of batting

Cutting

For 1 Windmill Block (Cut 15 Total.)

Refer to "Making the Blocks" and "Changing the Values" on page 55 before cutting the Windmill blocks.

From the medium scraps, cut:
2 squares, 5½" x 5½"

From the dark scraps, cut:
1 square, 5½" x 5½"

From the light scraps, cut:
1 square, 5½" x 5½"

For Sashing, Strips, Borders, and Corner Squares

From the purple-and-white print, cut:
2 strips, 7½" x 63", from the *lengthwise* grain
2 strips, 7½" x 53", from the *lengthwise* grain
2 strips, 13" x 42"; crosscut into 6 squares, 13" x 13". Cut each square into quarters diagonally to yield 24 side triangles.
2 strips, 7" x 42"; crosscut into 6 squares, 7" x 7". Cut each square in half diagonally to yield 12 corner triangles.

From the dark green print, cut:
12 strips, 1½" x 42"

From the light green print, cut:
2 strips, 4½" x 61", from the *lengthwise* grain

From the dark purple fabric, cut:
1 strip, 7½" x 42"; crosscut into 4 squares, 7½" x 7½"
8 strips, 2½" x 42"

Making the Blocks

In my quilt, the value placement in the Windmill blocks varies from one block to the next. The first block on the left below uses a medium value for the large windmill blades, dark for the center, and light for the small side triangles. The instructions are written for this block. If you'd like to change the positions of the values, see "Changing the Values" below.

CHANGING THE VALUES

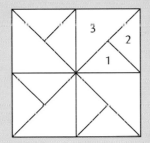

Cutting for one block:

Fabric 1 (small inner triangles): 1 square, 5½" x 5½"

Fabric 2 (small side triangles): 1 square, 5½" x 5½"

Fabric 3 (large triangles): 2 squares, 5½" x 5½"

When joining the small triangles cut from fabrics 1 and 2, always sew with fabric 2 on top as the paired units are fed under the presser foot, and always begin sewing at the right-angle corner.

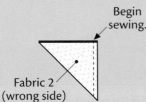

Begin sewing.

Fabric 2 (wrong side)

1. Refer to "Making Four Identical Three-in-a-Square Triangle Units" (page 14). When joining the paired quarter-square triangles, make sure the light fabric is on top as the units are fed into the machine.

2. Carefully arrange the units from step 1 as shown below. Sew the pieces of each block together in rows and press the seam allowances open. Sew the rows together and press the seam allowances open.

  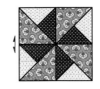

3. Repeat steps 1 and 2 to make 15 blocks.

Assembling the Quilt Top

1. Arrange the Windmill blocks, side triangles, and corner triangles into three vertical panels. Referring to "Diagonal Sets" (page 16), align the corners of the triangles with the corners of the blocks and sew together. Press the seam allowances toward the triangles. Trim the triangle points even with the edge of the blocks. Matching the seams of the units, join the units into panels. Press the seam allowances open. Add the corner triangles to the panels and press the seam allowances outward.

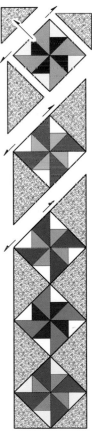

Make 3.

2. Trim the panels on all four sides, leaving a ¼" seam allowance beyond the block points.

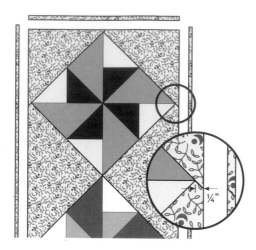

3. Measure the length of the three panels. If they differ, try to make adjustments using the average as the length.

4. Cut four of the dark green 1½"-wide strips into two equal lengths. Using a diagonal seam, sew each of the eight half strips to a remaining full-length strip.

5. Trim four of the pieced dark green strips to the length determined in step 3. Cut the two light green 4½" x 61" strips to the same length. Sew a dark green strip to each long side of a light green strip. Press toward the dark green fabric. Make two panels.

6. Arrange the three block panels and the two green panels as shown in the quilt diagram. Join the vertical rows. Press the seam allowances toward the dark green fabric.

7. Using the four remaining dark green pieced strips and referring to "Borders with Butted Corners" (page 17), add the side inner borders, and then the top and bottom inner borders. Press the seam allowances toward the borders.

Make 2.

8. Referring to "Borders with Corner Squares" (page 18), add the purple-and-white outer borders, including the dark purple 7½" squares. Press the seam allowances outward.

Finishing the Quilt

1. Cut the backing fabric across the grain into two equal pieces. Remove the selvages. Sew these pieces together along the lengthwise grain to create the quilt back. Press the seam open. The seam will run vertically on the quilt.

2. Layer and baste the quilt (page 19).

3. Hand or machine quilt as desired.

4. Refer to "Binding" (page 20) to use the dark purple 2½"-wide strips to bind the quilt.

5. Make and attach a label to your quilt.

hot stars over TEXAS

Made by Lynn Roddy Brown

Finished quilt: 66½" x 66½" – Finished block: 12" x 12"

I started this quilt with some black-with-white fabric from my stash. After making four Star blocks, I went fabric shopping. I wanted an assortment of backgrounds for the blocks so I bought white-with-black prints. After making several blocks with the new fabrics, I decided I liked the blocks with lighter backgrounds better. The four original blocks didn't even make it into the quilt. They've been added to my stash of leftovers and spare parts, waiting for another opportunity to appear in a quilt.

I used nine different reds and nine different yellows in this quilt. If you don't have enough fabric in your stash, consider using fat eighths or trading 5½" or 6" squares with your quilting friends.

Materials

Yardage is based on 42"-wide fabric.

2⅛ yards of black-and-gray polka-dot fabric for blocks, sashing squares, and borders

1⅓ yards *total* of white-with-black scraps for blocks and side and corner units

1 yard *total* of red scraps for blocks, sashing, and sashing squares*

1 yard *total* of yellow scraps for blocks and sashing**

⅞ yard *total* of black-with-white scraps for borders

⅝ yard of black tone-on-tone fabric for binding

4½ yards of fabric for backing

75" x 75" piece of batting

* *You can use 9 fat eighths if desired.*

**You can use 8 fat eighths and 1 fat quarter if desired.*

Cutting

From the white-with-black scraps, cut:
27 squares, 5½" x 5½" (9 matching sets of 3)
14 squares, 5½" x 5½"
12 squares, 4½" x 4½"

From the red scraps, cut:
18 squares, 5½" x 5½" (9 matching pairs)
32 strips, 1½" x 4½"
12 strips, 1½" x 12½"
16 squares, 1½" x 1½"

From the yellow scraps, cut:
18 squares, 5½" x 5½" (9 matching pairs)
16 strips, 1½" x 4½"
24 strips, 1½" x 12½"

From the black-and-gray polka-dot fabric, cut:
2 strips, 4½" x 70", from the *lengthwise* grain
2 strips, 4½" x 62", from the *lengthwise* grain
32 squares, 5½" x 5½"
20 squares, 1½" x 1½"

From black-with-white scraps, cut:
48 squares, 4½" x 4½"

From the black tone-on-tone fabric, cut:
7 strips, 2½" x 42"

Making the Star Blocks

For each Star block, you'll need:

- 2 matching red squares, 5½" x 5½"
- 2 matching yellow squares, 5½" x 5½"
- 3 matching white-with-black squares, 5½" x 5½"
- 2 black-and-gray polka-dot squares, 5½ x 5½"

1. Pair two white-with-black squares with black-and-gray polka-dot squares. Referring to "Making Two Identical Half-Square-Triangle Units" (page 11), make two identical pieced squares from each. Press the seam allowances toward the black-and-gray polka dot fabric and trim the units to 4½" square. Make four.

Make 4.

2. Using two yellow squares, one red square, and one white-with-black square, refer to "Making Four Identical Three-in-a-Square Triangle Units" (page 14). When joining the paired quarter-square triangles, the white-with-black fabric should be on top as the units are fed into the machine. Make four.

Make 4.

3. Trim the remaining red square to 4½" x 4½". Carefully arrange the units as shown. Sew the units together in rows. Press the seam allowances as shown below. Sew the rows together and press the seam allowances open.

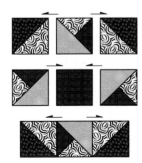

4. Repeat steps 1–3 to make a total of nine Star blocks.

Making the Side and Corner Units

1. Pair 14 assorted white-with-black 5½" squares with the remaining 14 black-and-gray polka-dot 5½" squares. Referring to "Making Two Identical Half-Square-Triangle Units" (page 11), make 28 pieced squares. Press the seam allowances toward the polka-dot fabric and trim the units to 4½" square.

Make 28.

2. For each side unit, select two units from step 1 and one white-with-black 4½" square. Arrange and sew together as shown; press the seam allowances toward the center. Make 12.

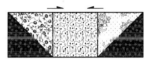

Make 12.

Assembling the Quilt Top

1. Arrange the blocks on your design wall in three horizontal rows of three blocks each. Add the side and corner units, making certain the black triangles are positioned correctly. Add the yellow sashing strips and red sashing squares to the design wall.

2. Sew the units and/or blocks together with the sashing strips in rows. Press toward the sashing. Sew the horizontal rows of sashing strips and squares together. Press toward the sashing. Join the rows and press the seam allowances toward the sashing.

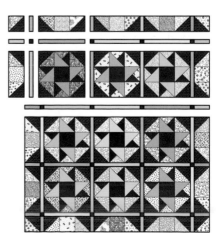

Adding the Borders

1. Using 36 of the black-with-white 4½" squares, sort them into 12 groups of three different squares. Arrange the squares as shown and sew together. Press toward the middle square. Make 12 units.

Make 12.

2. Sew three units from step 1, two black-with-white 4½" squares, and four red 1½" x 4½" strips to make a side border. Press toward the red sashing. Make two.

Make 2.

3. Sew three red 1½" x 12½" strips, two red 1½" x 4½" strips, and four black-and-gray polka-dot 1½" squares to make a strip as shown. Press toward the red strips. Make two strips.

Make 2.

4. Join the strips to the side borders. Press toward the red strip.

Make 2.

5. Sew three units from step 1, four black-with-white 4½" squares, and six red 1½" x 4½" strips to make a top border as shown. Press toward the red fabric. Repeat to make a bottom border.

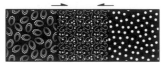

Make 2.

6. Sew three red 1½" x 12½" strips, four red 1½" x 4½" strips, and six black-and-gray polka-dot 1½" squares to make a narrow top border strip as shown. Press toward the red strips. Repeat to make a bottom border strip.

Make 2.

7. Join the top red strip to the top border strip. Press toward the red strip. Repeat to make the bottom border.

Make 2.

8. Sew the border units from step 4 to the sides of the quilt top. Press toward the border. Sew the border rows from step 6 to the top and bottom edges of the quilt top. Press toward the border.

9. Referring to "Borders with Butted Corners" (page 17), add the black-and-gray polka-dot outer borders to the sides using the two 4½" x 62" strips. Press the seam allowances toward the border. Using the black-and-gray polka-dot 4½" x 69" strips, add the top and bottom borders. Press toward the borders.

Finishing the Quilt

1. Cut the backing fabric across the grain into two equal pieces. Remove the selvages. Sew these pieces together along the lengthwise grain to create the quilt back. Press the seam open. The seam can run vertically or horizontally.

2. Layer and baste the quilt (page 19).

3. Hand or machine quilt as desired.

4. Refer to "Binding" (page 20) to use the black-tone-on-tone 2½"-wide strips to bind the quilt.

5. Make and attach a label to your quilt.

CROW'S nest

Made by Lynn Roddy Brown

Finished quilt: 67½" x 85½" – Finished block: 9" x 9"

If you want to use up scraps, here's your chance. Each Crow's Nest block includes 21 different fabrics, which makes for a very scrappy quilt. To make the blocks, I used a bag of half-square-triangle units from a block swap and my box of 1½" strips. You can also piece all of the units from Charm squares measuring 5" square. The block is made in two different value placements. By alternating the blocks with opposite values in the quilt setting, secondary patterns are created. Various patterns emerge depending on how you look at the quilt. The secondary patterns are what make this quilt so interesting.

Materials

Yardage is based on 42"-wide fabric.

2⅞ yards *total* of medium/dark scraps for blocks

2⅞ yards *total* of light scraps for blocks

2⅜ yards of dark green print for outer border

⅞ yard of light green fabric for inner border

⅔ yard of navy striped fabric for binding*

5¾ yards of fabric for backing

76" x 94" piece of batting

*For bias binding, you'll need 1¼ yards to make a total length of 318".

Cutting

From the medium/dark scraps, cut:
72 squares, 4¼" x 4¼"
67 strips, 1½" x 20"
22 squares, 3½" x 3½"

From the light scraps, cut:
72 squares, 4¼" x 4¼"
68 strips, 1½" x 20"
17 squares, 3½" x 3½"

From the light green fabric, cut:
7 strips, 3½" x 42"

From the dark green print, cut:
4 strips, 5½" x 78", cut on the *lengthwise* grain

From the navy striped fabric, cut:
8 strips, 2½" x 42"

Making the Block Units

1. Select a light and a medium/dark 4¼" square. Referring to "Making Two Identical Half-Square-Triangle Units" (page 11), make two units from the pair of squares. Press the seam allowances toward the medium/dark fabric and trim the units to 3½" square. Make 144 units.

Make 144.

2. Select three 1½" x 20" strips, one medium/dark and two light. Sew the light strips to each side of the medium/dark strip. Referring to "Rail Blocks from Strip Sets" (page 14), make five units, 3½" x 3½". Repeat to make 23 strip sets and 114 units.

Make 114.

3. Repeat step 2, selecting one light and two medium/dark 1½" x 20" strips. Sew the medium/dark strips to each side of the light strip. Make five units, 3½" x 3½". Repeat to make 22 strip sets and 106 units.

Make 106.

Making the Blocks

For this quilt you'll need 18 of block A and 17 of block B. The difference between the blocks is determined by the placement of the values.

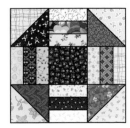

Block A

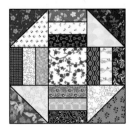

Block B

1. Select four different half-square-triangle units, four different rail units (light, dark, light), and one medium/dark 3½" square. Arrange the units into three rows as shown below. Make certain the values are positioned correctly.

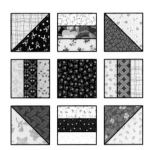

2. Sew the units together in rows. Press all seams toward the rail units. Sew the rows together, carefully matching the seams. Press the final seam allowances outward. Make 18 total of block A.

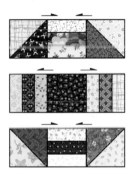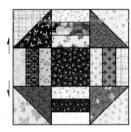

Make 18.

3. Select four different half-square-triangle units, four different rail units (dark, light, dark), and one light 3½" square. Arrange into three rows as shown below. Make certain the values in the units are positioned correctly. Sew the units together in rows. Press all seams toward the rail units. Sew the rows together, carefully matching the seams. Press the final seam allowances outward. Make 17 total of block B.

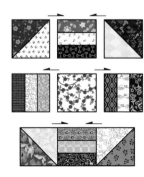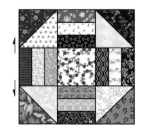

Make 17.

Assembling the Quilt Top

1. Arrange the blocks into seven horizontal rows of five blocks each, referring to the quilt diagram below. Alternate blocks A and B from row to row, with the top and bottom rows beginning and ending with block A.

2. Check the seam allowances and consider turning the blocks so that the seams of one block will butt with the seams in the next block. Sew the horizontal rows. Press the seams open.

3. Join the rows. Press the seams open.

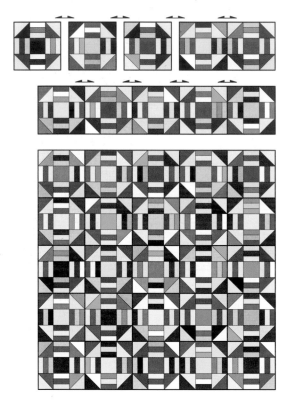

Adding the Borders

For the pieced border to fit, the quilt top should measure 45½" x 63½". Make adjustments by taking in or letting out seam allowances slightly, if necessary.

Making the Corner Blocks

1. Select one half-square-triangle unit, two different rail units (light, dark, light), and one medium/dark 3½" square. Arrange into two rows as shown below. Make certain the values in the units are positioned correctly.

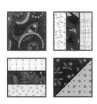

2. Sew the units together in rows. Press both seam allowances toward the rail units. Sew the rows together, carefully matching the seams. Press the final seam open. Make four corner blocks.

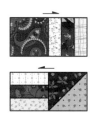

Make 4.

Making the Border Units

Each border unit is made of three rail units. You'll need 14 border units starting and ending with a dark strip and 10 units starting and ending with a light strip. For the border to fit, all units must measure 3½" x 9½".

1. Arrange two (dark, light, dark) rail units and one (light, dark, light) rail unit as shown below. Join the blocks and press all the seams in one direction. Make 14.

   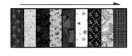

Make 14.

2. Arrange two (light, dark, light) rail units and one (dark, light, dark) rail unit as shown below. Join the blocks and press all the seams in one direction. Make 10.

   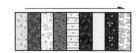

Make 10.

3. For the side borders, use four border units from step 1 and three border units from step 2. Alternate the units as shown below, starting and ending with units with dark ends. Make sure that the seam allowances are all facing the same direction. The border should measure 3½" x 63½". Make two.

Make 2.

4. For the top and bottom borders, use three border units from step 1 and two border units from step 2. Alternate the units as shown, starting and ending with units with dark ends. Make sure the seam allowances are all facing the same direction. The border should measure 3½" x 45½".

Make 2.

5. Sew two light green 3½"-wide strips together end to end using a diagonal seam. Press the seams open. Make two for the side borders. To make the top and bottom light green borders, cut one of the 3½"-wide strips into two equal lengths. Using a diagonal seam, sew these half strips to the remaining full-length light green strips. Press the seams open.

6. Trim the light green side borders to a length of 63½". Place a pieced side border on a light green border, right sides together. Position the seam allowances so that they'll be pressed down, toward the bottom of the finished quilt. Join the pieced border to the light green border. Press toward the light green border. Repeat to make the second side border.

7. Trim the light green top and bottom borders to a length of 45½". Place the pieced top border on a light green border, right sides together. Position the seam allowances so that they'll be facing away from the presser foot of your sewing machine. Join the pieced border to the light green border. Press toward the light green border. Repeat to make the bottom border.

8. Sew the two side borders from step 6 to the quilt. Press toward the light green borders.

9. Sew a corner block to each end of the top and bottom borders, making certain the corner blocks are positioned correctly. Press toward the borders. Add the top and bottom borders to the quilt. Press the seams toward the borders.

10. Refer to "Borders with Butted Corners" (page 17) to add the dark green outer borders.

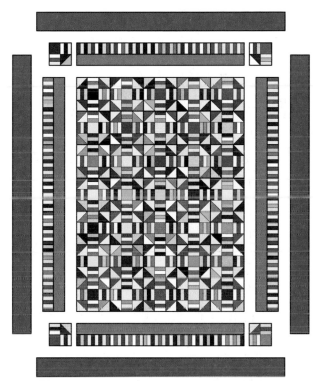

Finishing the Quilt

1. Cut the backing fabric across the grain into two equal pieces. Remove the selvages. Sew these pieces together along the lengthwise grain to create the quilt back. Press the seam open. The seam will run vertically on the quilt.

2. Layer and baste the quilt (page 19).

3. Hand or machine quilt as desired.

4. Refer to "Binding" (page 20) to use the navy striped 2½"-wide strips to bind the quilt.

5. Make and attach a label to your quilt.

hourglass and rail SURPRISE

Made by Lynn Roddy Brown
Finished quilt: 70½" x 70½" — Finished blocks: 6" x 6" — Finished rectangular Rail block: 6" x 7"

I didn't start out to make a medallion quilt. My inspiration was a picture of an antique quilt with alternating Hourglass and Rail blocks. I knew I had bags of both blocks that were leftovers from block swaps and other projects. I was sure that making the quilt would be quick and easy. However, when I started working on the design wall, I wasn't pleased with the results and began moving the blocks around. Even though I didn't use most of the already-made blocks, they helped me design this quilt. When I viewed them on the design wall, I decided that I wanted all of the Hourglass blocks to be red. Those extra blocks are now back in my stash, ready to provide inspiration for a future quilt.

For this project, I chose very light fabrics, reds, and very dark blues, greens, purples, and browns. The strong contrast in value along with the color placement created a less-scrappy quilt with an obvious pattern. The entire top for this quilt can be easily made using fat quarters, fat eighths, or scraps. I have a box of 2½" strips of varying lengths in my stash. I put these to good use.

Materials

Yardage is based on 42"-wide fabric.

3 yards *total* of light print scraps for Rail blocks, half-square Log Cabin blocks, Hourglass blocks, setting triangles, and borders

2⅛ yards *total* of dark blue, green, purple, and brown print scraps for Rail blocks, Half Log Cabin blocks, and borders

1⅛ yards *total* of assorted red prints for Rail and Hourglass blocks

⅔ yard of blue-and-brown print for binding

4⅞ yards of fabric for backing

79" x 79" piece of batting

Cutting

From the light prints, cut:

13 squares, 7½" x 7½"

12 squares, 2½" x 2½"

12 rectangles, 2½" x 4½"

16 rectangles, 2½" x 6½" (4 matching pairs and 8 random)

32 rectangles, 2½" x 7½"* (16 matching pairs)

2½"-wide strips of random lengths to total 380"**

3 squares, 11" x 11"; cut into quarters diagonally to yield 12 setting triangles

2 squares, 6½" x 6½"; cut in half diagonally to yield 4 corner triangles

From the dark blue, green, purple, and brown prints, cut:

12 squares, 2½" x 2½"

12 rectangles, 2½" x 4½"

28 rectangles, 2½" x 6½" (8 matching pairs and 12 random)

2½"-wide strips of random lengths to total 752"**

From the red prints, cut:

13 squares, 7½" x 7½"

4 rectangles, 2½" x 6½"

16 rectangles, 2½" x 7½"*

(continued)

From the blue-and-brown print, cut:

8 strips, 2½" x 42"

*Wait to cut the 2½" x 7½" rectangles until you're ready to add the second border.

**Lengths can range from about 6" to 14".

Making the Center Rail Blocks

1. Sew a light 2½" x 6½" rectangle to each long side of a red 2½" x 6½" rectangle; press toward the red fabric. Make four using the matching pairs.

Make 4.

2. Sew a dark 2½" x 6½" rectangle to each long side of a light 2½" x 6½" rectangle; press toward the dark fabric. Make eight using the matching pairs.

Make 8.

Making the Hourglass Blocks

For each set of two blocks you'll need a red 7½" square and a light 7½" square. Set aside two contrasting red squares to be used for the corner blocks in the second border.

1. Refer to "Making Two Identical Half-Square-Triangle Units" (page 11). Pair a light square with a red square. Cut the paired fabrics diagonally to form two triangles. Sew the diagonal seams of the triangle pairs; press toward the red fabric to make two identical half-square-triangle units. Do not trim.

2. Place the two half-square-triangle units right sides together, aligning the edges and butting the opposing seams. Check to make certain the light sides of the units are on opposite sides of

the nested seam. Cut the nested pair diagonally across the seam. Before moving the units from the mat, place one pin in each unit to hold the pieces together. Sew the seam and press the seam allowances open.

3. Trim the Hourglass blocks to 6½" square by placing the 45° line of a small square ruler along one of the seam lines. Position the 3¼" mark of the ruler on the unit center and trim the two adjacent sides. Rotate the unit so the trimmed edges are under the ruler on the 6½" mark. Trim the remaining sides.

Trim units to 6½" square.

4. Repeat steps 1–3 until you have 22 Hourglass blocks. One of the blocks will be extra.

Making the Half Log Cabin Blocks

1. Sew a light 2½" square to a dark 2½" square. Press the seam allowances toward the light fabric.

2. Place the unit from step 1 on top of a light 2½" x 4½" rectangle with right sides together. Position the unit so the light 2½" square feeds into the sewing machine first. Sew and press the seam allowances toward the light fabric.

Start sewing here.

3. Place a dark 2½" x 4½" rectangle on top of the unit from step 2 with right sides together so that the dark rectangle is on top of the seam between the light pieces. Sew and press seam allowances toward the light fabric.

4. Place a dark 2½" x 6½" rectangle on top of the unit from step 3 with right sides together and positioned as shown. Sew and press seam allowances toward the light fabric.

5. Repeat steps 1–4 until you have completed 12 Half Log Cabin blocks.

Making the Quilt Center

1. Using a design wall and referring to the assembly diagram, start in the center and arrange nine Hourglass blocks, the twelve Rail blocks, four Half Log Cabin blocks, and the side setting triangles into diagonal rows.

2. Sew the blocks and side setting triangles into diagonal rows, referring to "Diagonal Sets" (page 16). Press the seam allowances open.

3. Join the rows and press the seam allowances open. Add the corner triangles. Press the seam allowances outward. Trim the quilt on all four sides leaving ¼" seam allowance. The center should measure 34½" x 34½".

First Border

1. Using straight seams, join dark 2½"-wide strips of random lengths end to end to make a border strip that measures approximately 36". Press the seam allowances open. Make eight.

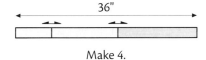

Make 8.

2. Repeat step 1 using light 2½"-wide strips of random lengths. Make four.

Make 4.

3. Sew a dark 2½" x 36" border strip to each long side of a light 2½" x 36" border strip. Press seam allowances toward the dark fabric. Trim the pieced border strip to be 34½" long. Make four.

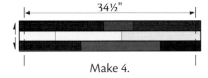

Make 4.

4. Referring to "Borders with Corner Squares" (page 18), add the borders using four Half Log Cabin blocks. Be sure the Half Log Cabin blocks are positioned correctly as shown in the quilt diagram.

Second Border

This pieced border uses Hourglass blocks, Rail blocks, and three-in-a-square triangle units in the corners. The quilt center with the first border added should measure 46½" x 46½". If your measurement differs, the length of the Rail blocks may be adjusted to make the border fit by cutting the rectangles slightly shorter or longer

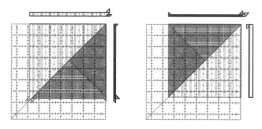

than 7½". Since there are four Rail blocks on each side, adding or subtracting ⅛" from each block will make a ½" difference in the border length.

1. Sew a light 2½" x 7½" rectangle to each long side of a red 2½" x 7½" rectangle; press toward the red fabric. Make 16.

Make 16.

2. Pair a red 7½" square with a contrasting red 7½" square. Referring to "Making Two Identical Half-Square-Triangle Units" (page 11), make two identical pieced squares from each. Press the seam allowances open. Don't trim the units.

3. Center each of the two red half-square-triangle units on a light 7½" square. Cut diagonally across the seam. Before moving the units from the mat, place one pin in each unit to hold them together. Sew the seam and press the seam allowances open. Make four.

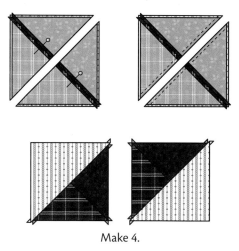

Make 4.

4. Trim the corner units to 6½" square by placing the 45° line of a small square ruler along the long seam line. Position the 3¼" mark of the ruler on the block center and trim the two adjacent sides. Rotate the unit so the trimmed edges are under the ruler on the 6½" mark. Trim the remaining sides.

5. Each pieced border unit uses four 7½" Rail blocks and three Hourglass blocks. Arrange the units as shown below. Join the blocks and press the seam allowances open.

6. Referring to "Borders with Corner Squares" (page 18), add the pieced borders using the four corner units from step 4. Be sure the corner units are positioned correctly, with the red half on the inside of the quilt as shown.

Third Border

1. Measure the width and length of the quilt top through the center, including the previously added borders. The quilt top should measure 58½" x 58½". Using straight seams, join dark 2½"-wide strips of random lengths end to end until the border strip measures 58½" (or your measured length). Press the seam allowances open. Make eight.

58½"

Make 8.

2. Repeat step 1 using light 2½"-wide strips. Make four.

58½"

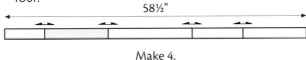

Make 4.

3. Sew a dark 2½" x 58½" border strip to each long side of a light 2½" x 58½" border strip (or use your measurement). Press seam allowances toward the dark fabric. Make four.

Make 4.

4. Referring to "Borders with Corner Squares" (page 18), add the borders using four Half Log Cabin blocks. Be sure the Half Log Cabin blocks are positioned correctly as shown.

Finishing the Quilt

1. Cut the backing fabric across the grain into two equal pieces. Remove the selvages. Sew these pieces together along the lengthwise grain to create the quilt back. Press the seam open. The seam can run vertically or horizontally.

2. Layer and baste the quilt (page 19).

3. Hand or machine quilt as desired.

4. Refer to "Binding" (page 20) to use the blue-and-brown 2½"-wide strips to bind the quilt.

5. Make and attach a label to your quilt.

LYNN SAYS: LEFTOVERS AND SPARE PARTS

For many years I've been a member of a Bee that swaps blocks for scrap quilts. Often the blocks I receive in the trade are not exactly what I had in mind. These blocks, along with units from mental-health sewing, from classes, abandoned projects, and samples, all go into a second stash that I call spare parts and leftovers. Also included are boxes of strips in 1½", 2", and 2½" widths and half-square-triangle units in a variety of sizes. This second stash often gives me a head start on a very scrappy quilt.

very varied VALUES

Made by Lynn Roddy Brown

Finished quilt: 73½" x 90½" – Finished block: 6" x 6"

This quilt began with a bag of Nine Patch blocks from a trade. As I put the blocks on the design wall, a few seemed to "glow." It took me awhile to realize that the glow came from the use of very light, clear fabrics. I searched my stash for more fabrics of this type and made additional blocks using five light squares and four medium squares. I then made blocks with five very dark squares and four medium squares. I made blocks and blocks trying to get the values just right. In the end, the original bag contained more blocks than it had when I started. Eventually most of those blocks went into another quilt.

When all of the blocks finally suited me, I added the green setting triangles. At that point I was stuck and the quilt top languished in my stash for five years before I added the final border. Fortunately, I was lucky and still had enough of the medium green to complete the zigzag border. Sometimes quilts just have to wait for the right inspiration.

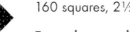

Materials

Yardage is based on 42"-wide fabric.

2⅞ yards of medium green print for blocks, setting triangles, and pieced border

2½ yards of dark green print for pieced border, outer border, and binding

1⅓ yards *total* of medium scraps for blocks

⅞ yard *total* of very light scraps for blocks

⅞ yard *total* of dark scraps for blocks

⅔ yard of dark blue floral for blocks

6 yards of fabric for backing

82" x 99" piece of batting

Cutting

From the medium scraps, cut:
252 squares, 2½" x 2½" (63 matching sets of 4)

From the dark scraps, cut:
160 squares, 2½" x 2½" (32 matching sets of 5)

From the very light clear scraps, cut:
155 squares, 2½" x 2½" (31 matching sets of 5)

From the dark blue floral, cut:
8 strips, 2½" x 42"

From the medium green print, cut:
16 strips, 2½" x 42"

7 squares, 11" x 11"; cut each square into quarters diagonally to yield 28 side triangles

2 squares, 6½" x 6½"; cut each square in half diagonally to yield 4 corner triangles

8 squares, 9¾" x 9¾"; cut each square into quarters diagonally to yield 32 border triangles

From the dark green print, cut:
9 squares, 9¾" x 9¾"; cut 7 of the squares into quarters diagonally to yield 28 border triangles and cut 2 of the squares in half diagonally to yield 4 corner triangles

9 strips, 3" x 42"

9 strips, 2½" x 42"

Making the Nine Patch Blocks

The Nine Patch blocks in this quilt consist of two different value configurations as shown. The O block pairs a very light fabric with a medium. The X block pairs a dark fabric with a medium. The medium fabric is in the same position in both blocks. Value placement is very important.

O block   X block

1. Select five matching light 2½" squares and four matching medium 2½" squares. Lay out the squares as shown. Make certain the light and medium fabrics are in the correct positions. Sew the squares together in rows; press the seam allowances toward the medium fabric. Join the rows and press. Make 31.

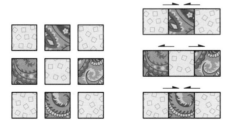

Make 31.

2. Select five matching dark 2½" squares and four matching medium 2½" squares. Lay out the squares as shown, making certain the light and medium fabrics are in the correct positions. Sew

the squares together in rows; press the seam allowances toward the dark fabric. Join the rows and press. Make 32.

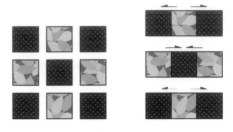

Make 32.

Making the Rail Blocks

Sew a medium green 2½" x 42" strip to each long side of a dark blue floral 2½" x 42" strip. Press the seams toward the medium green fabric. Make a total of eight strip sets and cut the strip sets into 48 total segments, 6½" wide.

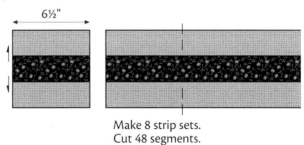

Make 8 strip sets.
Cut 48 segments.

Assembling the Quilt Top

1. Working on a design wall and referring to the quilt diagram, arrange the X Nine Patch blocks, the O Nine Patch blocks, and the Rail blocks in diagonal rows. Note that the Nine Patch blocks alternate. The first and last rows begin and end with an X block. Alternate the direction of the Rail blocks to form a diagonal pattern.

2. Add the side triangles to the layout. Referring to "Diagonal Sets" (page 16), join the blocks and side triangles in diagonal rows. Press the seam allowances toward the Rail blocks. Join the

rows and press the seam allowances open. Add the corner triangles; press the seam allowances outward.

3. Trim the quilt on all four sides, leaving a ¼" seam allowance.

4. Sewing the triangles for the pieced border is much easier if the triangle points are trimmed. To trim the points, you can use a special point-trimmer ruler or a rotary ruler with ⅛" marks. Align the ⅜" line with a short edge of the triangle. Position the ruler so the corner is just touching the long edge of the triangle as shown. Trim the point. Rotate the triangle and trim the second point. Repeat for all 32 medium green print triangles and 28 dark green print triangles.

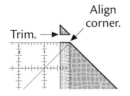

Trim. → Align corner.

5. Each pieced border starts and ends with a medium green print triangle. To join the border triangles, place a medium green print triangle right sides together with a dark green print triangle as shown.

Notice the position of the ¼" seam line in relation to the trimmed point. Sew the seam and press open.

6. Join seven medium green print triangles and six dark green print triangles for the top/bottom border; make two. Piece a side border using nine medium green print triangles and eight dark green triangles; make two.

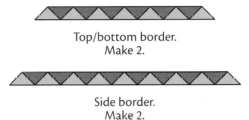

Top/bottom border.
Make 2.

Side border.
Make 2.

7. Add the side borders using pins and a steam iron if necessary to adjust the fit. Press the seam allowances open. Add the top and bottom borders. Press the seam allowances open. Add the dark green corner triangles and press outward.

8. To make the dark green side borders, cut one 3" x 42" strip into two equal lengths. Using diagonal seams, join two full width strips and a half strip to make each side border. Using a diagonal seam, join two dark green 3" x 42" border strips for the top outer border and two for the bottom outer border. Referring to "Borders with Butted Corners" (page 17), add the outer borders.

Finishing the Quilt

1. Cut the backing fabric across the grain into two equal pieces. Remove the selvages. Sew these pieces together along the lengthwise grain to create the quilt back. Press the seams open. The seam will run vertically on the quilt.

2. Layer and baste the quilt (page 19).

3. Hand or machine quilt as desired.

4. Refer to "Binding" (page 20) to use the dark green print 2½"-wide strips to bind the quilt.

5. Make and attach a label to your quilt.

NINE PATCH trip

Made by Lynn Roddy Brown
Finished quilt: 50" x 64" — Finished block: 5" x 5"

I've always liked Trip around the World quilts. For this simplified version, I alternated Framed Nine Patch blocks with plain squares. The consistent placement of very light values in the Framed Nine Patch blocks create chains. The block directions are written using 1½" x 21" strips, which can be easily cut from fat eighths. If you want to use tiny scraps instead, you could piece the nine-patch units from individual 1½" squares.

Materials

Yardage is based on 42"-wide fabric.

2 yards of red print for setting triangles and borders

1 yard of medium blue print for blocks

1 fat eighth *each* of 8 dark prints for blocks*

⅞ yard *total* of very light scraps for blocks**

20 assorted purple squares, 5½" x 5½"

12 assorted red squares, 5½" x 5½"

3 assorted yellow squares, 5½" x 5½"

⅝ yard of green print for binding

3½ yards of fabric for backing

58" x 72" piece of batting

*Or 1½" x 42" strips or scraps at least 4" x 21".

**You'll need 1½"-wide strips at least 21" long.

Cutting

From the very light scraps, cut:
36 strips, 1½" x 21"; crosscut 4 strips into a total of 8 strips, 1½" x 10½"

From *each* of the 8 dark prints, cut:
2 strips, 1½" x 21" (16 total)

From the medium blue print, cut:
8 strips, 3½" x 42"; crosscut into:
    8 strips, 3½" x 21"
    96 rectangles, 1½" x 3½"

From the red print, cut:
2 strips, 4" x 62", from the *lengthwise* grain
2 strips, 4" x 55", from the *lengthwise* grain
6 squares, 9¼" x 9¼"; cut each square into quarters diagonally to yield 24 side triangles
2 squares, 5½" x 5½"; cut each square in half diagonally to yield 4 corner triangles

From the green print, cut:
6 strips, 2½" x 42"

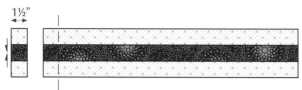

Making the Blocks

The center nine-patch units for the blocks came from a trade and were made using two fabrics each. I added framing strips using the same medium blue print for each block. Since I was unable to match the light fabrics in the traded blocks, I used random light squares. The most important thing is that the lights are very light.

1. Select one dark 1½" x 21" strip and two *matching* light 1½" x 21" strips. Sew the light strips to each side of the dark strip. Press the seam allowances toward the dark strip. Trim and square up the left edge; cut 12 segments, 1½" wide.

1½"

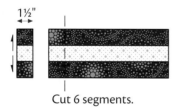

Cut 12 segments.

2. Select a dark 1½" x 21" strip that matches the dark strip used in step 1 and cut it into two strips, 1½" x 10½". Sew the dark strips to each side of a light 1½" x 10½" strip. Press the seam allowances toward the dark strip. Trim and square up the left edge; cut 6 segments, 1½" wide.

1½"

Cut 6 segments.

3. Arrange the segments from steps 1 and 2 into a nine-patch unit as shown. Pin and sew the segments together, matching seams. Press the seam allowances open. Make six.

Make 6.

4. Repeat steps 1–3 to make a total of 48 nine-patch units.

5. Sew a light 1½" x 21" strip to each side of a medium blue 3½" x 21" strip. Press the seam allowances toward the medium blue fabric. Trim and square up the left edge; cut 1½"-wide segments. Repeat until you've made a total of eight strip sets and have 96 segments.

1½"

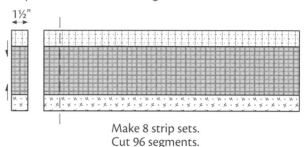

Make 8 strip sets.
Cut 96 segments.

6. Sew a medium blue 1½" x 3½" rectangle to the top and bottom of each of the 48 nine-patch units. Press toward the blue rectangles.

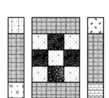

Make 48.

7. Sew two segments from step 5 to the sides of the unit as shown. Pin and sew the segments together, matching seams. Press the seam allowances outward. Repeat until you have a total of 48 Framed Nine Patch blocks.

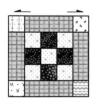

Make 48.

Assembling the Quilt Top

1. Using a design wall and referring to the quilt diagram, start in the center and arrange the Framed Nine Patch blocks, plain squares, and side setting triangles into diagonal rows. Scatter the identical Framed Nine Patch blocks across the surface of the quilt.

2. Sew the blocks and side setting triangles into diagonal rows, referring to "Diagonal Sets" (page 16). Press the seam allowances open.

3. Join the rows and press the seam allowances open. Add the corner triangles; press the seam allowances outward.

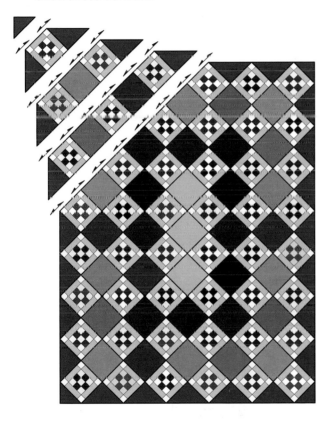

4. Trim the quilt on all four sides, leaving a ¼" seam allowance beyond the block points.

5. Referring to "Borders with Butted Corners" (page 17), add the red print outer borders to the sides using the two 4" x 62" strips. Press the seam allowances toward the borders. Add the red print 4" x 55" strips to the top and bottom. Press toward the borders.

Finishing the Quilt

1. Cut the backing fabric across the grain into two equal pieces. Remove the selvages. Sew these pieces together along the lengthwise grain to create the quilt back. Press the seams open. The seam will run horizontally on the quilt.

2. Layer and baste the quilt (page 19).

3. Hand or machine quilt as desired.

4. Refer to "Binding" (page 20) to use the green 2½"-wide strips to bind the quilt.

5. Make and attach a label to your quilt.

LYNN SAYS: SHOPPING STRATEGY FOR SCRAP QUILTS

Shopping for scrap quilts is very different than shopping for a planned project using a limited number of fabrics. The sale table is a great place to hunt for treasures. These are the fabrics that didn't sell well. They often have great visual texture, unusual patterns, and not-so-pleasing colors. Look for medium to dark fabrics that don't have large areas of very light colors.

Avoid fabrics that have only one color, known to quilters as tone-on-tone prints. These fabrics may be beautiful, but generally they don't add much interest and you probably already have lots of these. Most quilters don't have enough light fabrics. These aren't very exciting, but you need them. I think of fabrics with white or beige backgrounds as lights and those with pastel backgrounds as medium lights.

Trading strips or squares of fabric with your quilting friends is an easy way to add variety to your stash. You'll get colors and textures you may not normally buy.

NINE PATCH boogie

Made by Francis (Fran) Urquhart; quilted by Sharon Dixon
Finished quilt: 75½" x 84½" – Finished blocks: 3" x 3" and 4½" x 4½"

Fran and I belong to a group that swaps blocks for scrap quilts. The 3" Nine Patch blocks Fran used in this quilt were from one of our trades. My quilt, "Nine Patch Trip," is shown previously (page 76). When I asked her how she pieced this quilt, she said she sewed the middle in rows, and then decided the quilt needed to be bigger and started adding to the sides. Fran did try to scatter blocks that were the same or similar colors but really did not stress over what went with each block. I think it's this randomness of value and color placement that makes this a great quilt.

If this quilt seems like too large a project, maybe you need to think of it in a different way. There are 504 Nine Patch blocks. If you use this quilt as mental-health sewing, you would only need to make about 10 blocks a week for a year. You can also make two blocks from two 5" charm squares (see page 12 for this method).

Materials

Yardage is based on 42"-wide fabric.

5⅔ yards *total* of medium/dark scraps for blocks*

5⅔ yards *total* of light scraps for blocks*

1⅓ yards of red tone-on-tone print for inner border and binding

5⅔ yards of fabric for backing

84" x 93" piece of batting

Your scraps should be at least 5" x 21" for the 3" blocks and 7" x 21" for the 4½" blocks. You'll need 3 matching strips of each fabric as indicated in the cutting list below.

Cutting

From the medium/dark scraps, cut:
189 strips, 1½" x 21" (in matching sets of 3)
66 strips, 2" x 21" (in matching sets of 3)

From the light scraps, cut:
189 strips, 1½" x 21" (in matching sets of 3)
66 strips, 2" x 21" (in matching sets of 3)

From the red tone-on-tone print, cut:
10 strips, 2" x 42"; crosscut 1 strip into 4 rectangles, 2" x 4½"
9 strips, 2½" x 42"

Making the 3"
Nine Patch Blocks

What makes this quilt interesting are the inconsistent values in the blocks. Some blocks are light and dark, some are light and medium, and some are medium and dark. The contrast in value within each block is the most important thing, not consistent values from block to block.

1. Select a set of three identical light or medium 1½" x 21" strips and a set of three identical medium/dark 1½" x 21" strips. Just be sure that you have contrasting values. Refer to "Making Nine Patch Blocks from Strip Sets" (page 13) to make four X blocks and four O blocks. (The difference between the blocks is determined by the placement of the values.) Press the seams as indicated.

X block.   O block.
Make 4.   Make 4.

2. Repeat step 1 to make a total of 252 X blocks and 252 O blocks.

Making the 9"
Nine Patch Blocks

1. Select five different 3" X blocks and four different 3" O blocks. Arrange the blocks as shown. Sew the blocks together in rows and press the seam allowances toward the X blocks. Sew the rows

together and press the seam allowances away from the center row. Make 28 large X blocks.

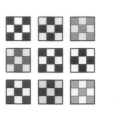 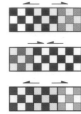

Large X block.
Make 28.

2. Repeat step 1 with five different O blocks and four different X blocks. Arrange the blocks as shown. Press the seam allowances toward the center row. Make 28 large O blocks.

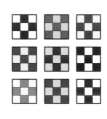 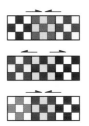

Large O block.
Make 28.

Making the 4½"
Nine Patch Blocks

1. Select a set of three identical light 2" x 21" strips and a set of three identical medium/dark 2" x 21" strips. Refer to "Making Nine Patch Blocks from Strip Sets" (page 13) to make three X blocks and three O blocks.

X block.   O block.
Make 3.   Make 3.

2. Repeat step 1 to make a total of 32 X blocks and 32 O blocks for the pieced border.

Assembling the Quilt Top

1. Arrange the 9" Nine Patch blocks into eight horizontal rows of seven blocks each, referring to the quilt diagram below. The X and O blocks alternate from row to row, with the top row beginning and ending with an X block.

2. Sew the horizontal rows. Press the seams open.

3. Join the rows. Press the seams open.

4. Sew 14 of the 4½" Nine Patch blocks together, alternating X and O blocks for the top border. Repeat for the bottom border.

5. Sew two red 2" x 42" strips together end to end, using a diagonal seam to make a top inner border. Press the seam allowances open. Repeat to make the bottom inner border.

6. Measure across the center of the quilt body and trim the red strips to this length for the top and bottom inner borders. Sew one strip to each of the Nine Patch border strips. Press the seam allowances toward the inner border. Attach the top and bottom borders. Press the seam allowances toward the inner border.

7. Referring to the quilt diagram, piece each side border using 18 border blocks and two red 2" x 4½" rectangles.

8. For each of the red inner side borders, sew two 2"-wide strips end to end using a diagonal seam. Cut the remaining 2" x 42" strip into two equal lengths. Sew these half strips to the ends of the side inner borders. Press the seams open. Measure lengthwise through the center of the quilt. Trim the inner borders to this measurement.

9. Sew the red inner side borders to the pieced side borders. Press the seam allowances toward the inner border.

10. Attach the side borders, making sure the horizontal inner borders are aligned with the red rectangles in the border. Press the seam allowances toward the inner border.

Finishing the Quilt

1. Cut the backing fabric across the grain into two equal pieces. Remove the selvages. Sew these pieces together along the lengthwise grain to create the quilt back. Press the seam open. The seam will run vertically on the quilt.

2. Layer and baste the quilt (page 19).

3. Hand or machine quilt as desired.

4. Refer to "Binding" (page 20) to use the red 2½"-wide strips to bind the quilt.

5. Make and attach a label to your quilt.

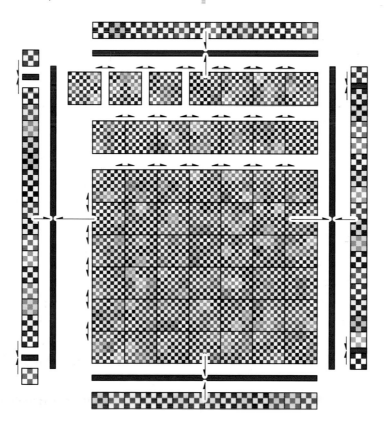

ARGYLE squares

Made by Lynn Roddy Brown with design help from Elizabeth (Liz) Broussard
Finished quilt: 54" x 71" — Finished block: 6" x 6"

Nine Patch and Four Patch blocks create the complex look of argyle socks in this quilt made of Civil War reproduction prints and shirtings. The first set of Nine Patch blocks that I made had an orange striped center. To give the quilt more structure and make it easier to see the pattern, I decided to make all of the Nine Patch blocks with orange centers and place the stripes at the same angle.

Once I had the Nine Patch and Four Patch blocks on the design wall, the pattern seemed incomplete. Pieced setting triangles would be a good solution, but the side triangles would need values opposite the top and bottom triangles, resulting in light edges on the sides and dark edges on the top and bottom. Because the quilt edges have both light and dark values, I fussy cut a dark orange striped print so the light edge of the stripe met the top and bottom and the dark edge met the sides.

Materials

Yardage is based on 42"-wide fabric.

2⅞ yards of dark orange striped print for border and binding*

1⅞ yards *total* of light shirting scraps for blocks and setting triangles**

1¾ yards *total* of medium/dark Civil War reproduction scraps for blocks and setting triangles**

1 fat quarter of light orange striped print for blocks

4 yards of fabric for backing

62" x 79" piece of batting

For bias binding, you'll need to add an additional ½ yard for a total length of 262". The width of the border is determined by the stripe. If the borders on your quilt will be wider than 6" and mitered, allow an additional ¼ yard.

**The scraps should include 20 different strips, 2½" x 21".*

Cutting

From the medium/dark scraps, cut:
20 different strips, 2½" x 21"
60 assorted squares, 3½" x 3½"
5 assorted squares, 6" x 6"

From the light scraps, cut:
20 different strips, 2½" x 21"
56 assorted squares, 3½" x 3½"
7 assorted squares, 6" x 6"

From the light orange striped print, cut:
5 strips, 2½" x 21"

From the dark orange striped print, cut:
4 strips, 6" x 74", from the *lengthwise* grain*
7 strips, 2½" x 42"

If you're using a striped print for the border, refer to "Fussy Cutting Stripes" (page 17).

Making the Nine Patch Blocks

The blocks are made in sets of seven identical blocks. Each block will have nine different fabrics. For each set of seven blocks, you'll need:

- 4 different light strips, 2½" x 21"
- 4 different medium/dark strips, 2½" x 21"
- 1 light orange striped strip, 2½" x 21"

1. Make three strip sets as shown below. Press toward the darker fabrics. Cut seven segments, 2½" wide, from each strip set.

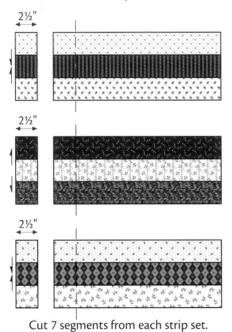

Cut 7 segments from each strip set.

2. Select one segment from each strip set and arrange the segments as shown. Pin and sew the segments together, matching seams. Press the seam allowances open.

Make 7.

3. Repeat steps 1 and 2 until you've completed 35 blocks.

Making the Four Patch Blocks

1. Select two different light 3½" squares and two different medium/dark 3½" squares. Arrange the squares as shown. Sew the squares together in

rows and press the seam allowances toward the lighter squares. Sew the rows together and press the seam allowances open.

 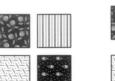

Make 24.

2. Repeat step 1 to make 24 blocks.

Making the Setting Triangles

The side setting triangles are pieced using dark 3½" squares and light triangles. The top and bottom setting triangles use light 3½" squares and dark triangles. The corner setting triangles are made from two half-square-triangle units cut in half.

1. Cut six light 6" squares into quarters diagonally to yield 24 quarter-square triangles.

2. Matching the corners, sew a light triangle to a medium/dark 3½" square. Press the seam allowances toward the triangle. Trim the point. Add a second light triangle as shown. Press the seam allowances outward. Do not trim. Make 12.

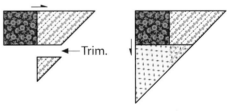

Make 12.

3. Cut four medium/dark 6" squares into quarters diagonally to yield 16 quarter-square triangles.

4. Matching the corners, sew a medium/dark triangle to a light 3½" square. Press the seam allowances toward the triangle. Trim the point. Add a second medium/dark triangle as shown. Press the seam allowances outward. Do not trim. Make eight.

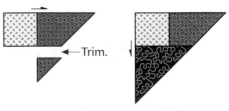

Make 8.

5. Pair the remaining medium/dark 6" square with the light 6" square. Referring to "Making Two Identical Half-Square-Triangle Units" (page 11), make two identical pieced squares. Do not trim. Press the seam allowances open. Cut each half-square-triangle unit in half diagonally across the seam to create four corner triangles.

Assembling the Quilt Top

1. Working on a design wall and referring to the quilt diagram, arrange the Nine Patch and Four Patch blocks in diagonal rows. Be certain the dark squares of the Four Patch blocks are positioned to create horizontal rows. I placed the Nine Patch blocks so that the striped squares in the center were all at the same angle. Add the setting triangles with dark squares to the sides. Add the setting triangles with light squares to the top and bottom.

2. Sew the blocks and side setting triangles into diagonal rows, referring to "Diagonal Sets" (page 16). Press the seam allowances open.

3. Join the rows and press the seam allowances open. Add the corner triangles, making certain the light side of each triangle aligns with the light edges of the quilt.

4. Trim the quilt on all four sides, leaving a 1/4" seam allowance.

5. Add the dark orange striped borders, referring to "Borders with Mitered Corners" (page 18).

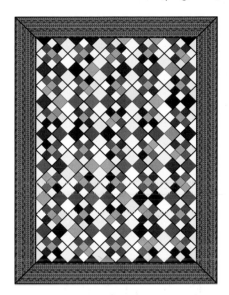

Finishing the Quilt

1. Cut the backing fabric across the grain into two equal pieces. Remove the selvages. Sew these pieces together along the lengthwise grain to create the quilt back. Press the seam allowance open. The seam will run horizontally across the quilt.

2. Layer and baste the quilt (page 19).

3. Hand or machine quilt as desired.

4. Refer to "Binding" (page 20) to use the dark orange 2½"-wide strips to bind the quilt.

5. Make and attach a label to your quilt.

buckeye BEAUTY

Made by Lynn Roddy Brown
Finished quilt: 66½" x 82½" — Finished block: 8" x 8"

I searched through my stash of so-called "ugly" fabric looking for strong visual textures and unusual colors to make the blocks for this quilt. When I chose two fabrics for a block, I made certain there was a contrast in value. Sometimes I used a combination of light with dark and other times it was light with medium or medium with dark. The number of fabrics, the varied prints, the inconsistent value contrast, and the alternating placement of values all work together to make this a very scrappy quilt.

Materials

Yardage is based on 42"-wide fabric.

2⅜ yards *total* of medium/dark scraps for blocks

2⅜ yards *total* of light scraps for blocks

2¼ yards of brown print for outer border

⅝ yard of teal fabric for inner border

⅔ yard of teal plaid for binding*

5½ yards of fabric for backing

75" x 91" piece of batting

For bias binding, you'll need 1 yard to make a total length of 310".

Cutting

From the medium/dark scraps, cut:
48 strips, 2½" x 11"*
48 squares, 5¼" x 5¼"*

From the light scraps, cut:
48 strips, 2½" x 11"*
48 squares, 5¼" x 5¼"*

From the teal fabric, cut:
7 strips, 2½" x 42"

From the brown print, cut:
4 strips, 7½" x 72", from the *lengthwise* grain

From the teal plaid, cut:
8 strips, 2½" x 42"

Cut one 5¼" square and one 2½" x 11" strip from the same fabric.

Making the Blocks

For this quilt you'll need 24 of block A and 24 of block B. Each block is made from two four-patch units and two half-square-triangle units. The difference between the blocks is determined by the placement of the values.

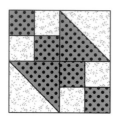 

Block A   Block B

1. Select one light and one medium/dark square, or two squares that contrast in value. Refer to "Making Two Identical Half-Square-Triangle Units" (page 11) to make two identical units from the pair of squares. Press the seam allowances toward the darker fabric and trim the units to 4½" square.

2. Select the two 2½" x 11" strips that match the fabrics used in step 1. Place the strips right sides together and sew along one long edge. Press toward the darker fabric. Cut the strip set into four 2½" segments.

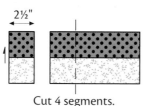

Cut 4 segments.

3. Place the segments from step 2 right sides together with seams butting. Use a straight pin to secure the seam; sew together and press the seam allowance open. Make two.

Make 2.

4. For block A, arrange the half-square-triangle units from step 1 and the four-patch units from step 3 as shown. Make sure the values in the units are positioned correctly. Sew the units together in rows. Press the seam allowances toward the four-patch unit. Sew the rows together, carefully matching the seams. Press the final seam allowances open. Repeat steps 1–4 to make a total of 24 of block A.

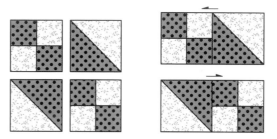

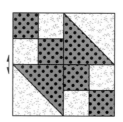

Make 24.

5. For block B, repeat steps 1–3. Arrange the half-square-triangle units from step 1 and the four-patch units from step 3 as shown. Make sure the values in the units are positioned correctly. Sew the units together in rows. Press the seam allowances toward the four-patch unit. Sew the rows together, carefully matching the seams. Press the final seam allowances open. Repeat to make a total of 24 of block B.

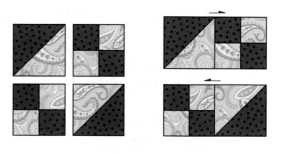

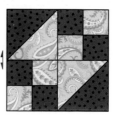

Make 24.

Assembling the Quilt Top

1. Arrange the blocks into eight horizontal rows of six blocks each, referring to the quilt diagram below. Alternate blocks A and B from row to row, with the top row beginning with a block A and ending with a block B. Make certain the blocks are turned so the four-patch units are created where the blocks meet.

2. Sew the blocks into horizontal rows. Press the seams open.

3. Join the rows. Press the seams open.

4. For each of the teal side inner borders, use two 2½" x 42" strips. Sew these strips end to end using a diagonal seam. Press the seams open. To make the top and bottom inner borders, cut one of the teal 2½" x 42" strips into two equal lengths. Using a diagonal seam, sew each half strip to a teal full-length strip. Press the seams open.

5. Refer to "Borders with Butted Corners" (page 17) to add the teal inner borders.

6. Add the brown print borders in the same manner using the 7½" x 72" strips.

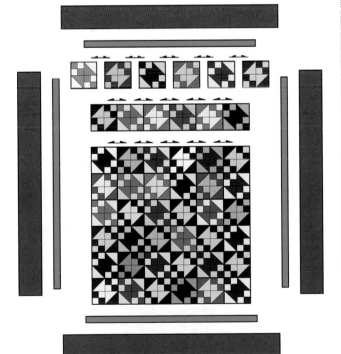

Finishing the Quilt

1. Cut the backing fabric across the grain into two equal pieces. Remove the selvages. Sew these pieces together along the lengthwise grain to create the quilt back. Press the seam open. The seam will run vertically on the quilt.

2. Layer and baste the quilt (page 19).

3. Hand or machine quilt as desired.

4. Refer to "Binding" (page 20) and use the teal plaid 2½"-wide strips to bind the quilt.

5. Make and attach a label to your quilt.

LYNN SAYS: GET A HEAD START

Sometimes it may seem that starting a new project will involve too many decisions. When that happens, my solution is to make simple blocks such as half-square-triangle or four-patch units. With scrap quilts, you don't need to know how the units will be used. This frees you to sew together any fabrics that you find pleasing. The fabric is in your stash. When you make blocks, the fabric is still in your stash—it's just changed form.

When I'm cutting yardage for projects and the fabric is pressed and on the cutting mat, I will often cut strips in 1½", 2", and 2½" widths to add to my strip boxes. These come in handy for strip piecing. A variety of fabric is already in the box. I don't need to pull 20 or more different fabrics to cut strips for a project. Precut rolls of 1½"- and 2½"-wide strips (Honey Buns and Jelly Rolls) can also be found in quilt stores.

baby blue BUCKEYE

Made by Janice Thompson and Lynn Roddy Brown, with design help from the Piecemakers

Finished quilt: 47" x 54½" – Finished block: 6" x 6"

My quilting friend Janice made these blocks out of 1930s reproduction prints. They all have a common light background, making value decisions easy. We began playing with the blocks on my design wall, but somehow the quilt wasn't working. We decided to take the blocks to our Friday Piecemakers meeting to get other opinions. I love that quilters are always willing to help and share ideas. At the meeting, we worked together to come up with this design, and our friend Sandra Weaver donated the perfect blue striped fabric for the inner border and binding.

This quilt is the least scrappy in the book, but it has several things that make it interesting. The asymmetrical blocks create strong diagonal lines that move the viewer's eye across the surface. The blocks are set four across and five down, in an unbalanced setting like many antique quilts that were made to fit a bed. In addition, Nine Patch blocks form where the blocks and sashing squares meet, and the medium to dark blocks appear to float above the very light surface.

Materials

Yardage is based on 42"-wide fabric.

2⅝ yards of very light print for blocks, sashing, sashing squares, and borders

1 fat eighth *each* of 20 medium/dark prints for blocks and sashing squares*

¾ yard of blue striped fabric for inner border and binding**

3⅓ yards for backing

55" x 63" piece of batting

*If you want to use scraps, you'll need 20 pieces, approximately 8" x 10".

**For bias binding and inner border, you'll need 1½ yards to make a total length of 215" for binding.

Cutting

From the light print, cut *from the lengthwise* grain:
2 strips, 6½" x 46"
2 strips, 6½" x 51"
2 strips, 2" x 36"
2 strips, 2" x 40"

From the remainder of the light print, cut:
3 strips, 4¼" x 42"; crosscut into 20 squares, 4¼" x 4¼"

10 strips, 2" x 42"; crosscut into:
    20 rectangles, 2" x 9"
    31 rectangles, 2" x 6½"
    6 squares, 2" x 2"

From *each* of the medium/dark scraps, cut:
1 square, 4¼" x 4¼" (20 total)
1 rectangle, 2" x 9" (20 total)

From *each* of 6 of the medium/dark scraps, cut:
1 square, 2" x 2" (6 total)

From the blue striped fabric, cut:
4 strips, 2" x 42"
6 strips, 2½" x 42"

Making the Blocks

1. Select one medium/dark 4¼" square and one light print 4¼"square. Refer to "Making Two Identical Half-Square-Triangle Units" (page 11) to make two identical units from the pair of squares. Press the seam allowances toward the dark fabric and trim the units to 3½" square.

2. Select the medium/dark 2" x 9" rectangle that matches the medium/dark square in step 1 and one light print 2" x 9" rectangle. Place the strips right sides together and sew along one long edge. Press toward the medium/dark fabric. Cut the strip set into four 2" segments.

2"

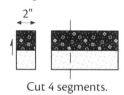

Cut 4 segments.

3. Pair the four segments. Place each pair right sides together with seams butting as shown. Use a straight pin to secure the seams. Sew together and press the seam allowances open.

Make 2.

4. Arrange the half-square-triangle units and the four-patch units as shown. Sew the units together in rows. Press the seam allowances toward the four-patch units. Sew the rows together, carefully matching the seams. Press the final seam allowances open. Repeat steps 1–4 to make a total of 20 blocks.

Make 20.

Assembling the Quilt Top

1. Working on a design wall, arrange the blocks in five horizontal rows of four blocks each. Referring to the quilt diagram, rotate the blocks to form the diagonal pattern as shown. Add the light print 2" x 6½" sashing strips, the light print 2" sashing squares, and the medium/dark 2" sashing squares to the design wall. The light print sashing squares will help keep the blocks aligned and the quilt square.

2. Sew the blocks and sashing strips together into rows. Press seam allowances toward the sashing. Sew the horizontal rows of sashing strips and sashing squares together. Press toward the sashing.

3. Join the rows. Press toward the sashing.

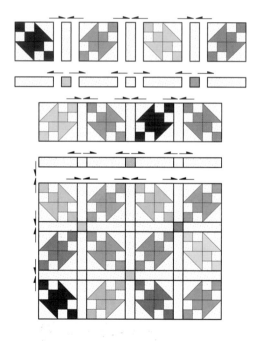

4. Refer to "Borders with Butted Corners" (page 17) to use the light print 2" x 40" strips for the side borders and the 2" x 36" strips for the top and bottom borders.

5. Add the blue striped borders using the four 2" x 42" strips.

6. Add the light print outer borders using the 6½" x 46" strips for the side borders and the 6½" x 51" strips for the top and bottom borders.

Finishing the Quilt

1. Cut the backing fabric across the grain into two equal pieces. Remove the selvages. Sew these pieces together along the lengthwise grain to create the quilt back. Press the seam open. The seam will run horizontally on the quilt.

2. Layer and baste the quilt (page 19).

3. Hand or machine quilt as desired.

4. Refer to "Binding" (page 20) to use the blue striped 2½"-wide strips to bind the quilt.

5. Make and attach a label to your quilt.

RESIDUAL CLAIMANT

Made by Lynn Roddy Brown, 71½" x 71½"

My husband, an economist, uses the term residual claimant to mean the person or thing that gets what's left.

When I went to Gwen Marston's "Liberated Quiltmaking" retreat in Michigan, I took my bags of unused blocks. This quilt was the result. The blocks range in size from 3" to 6" and include: Triple Four Patch, Four Patch, Nine Patch, and half-square-triangle units. I only made one 6" Four Patch block for this quilt. All of the rest came from the bags.

I had great fun playing on the design wall with my leftovers and spare parts. I haven't provided instructions for this quilt; I'm hoping it will inspire you to create your very own "Residual Claimant."

about the AUTHOR

Lynn Roddy Brown is a sixth-generation Texan who has always loved to sew. She took her first sewing lessons at the age of eight at the local Singer sewing-machine shop. When she was 10, she won the Singer regional dressmaking contest and received a sewing machine as her prize.

There was one beautiful quilt in her home as Lynn was growing up, made by Lynn's great-grandmother as a wedding gift for her parents. This quilt, which now belongs to Lynn, kindled a lifelong interest in quilting. In the early 1970s, she began tearing pictures of quilts from magazines and did some patchwork with templates, but it was not until 1989 when she lived in Rochester, New York, that she began to quilt seriously.

For the past 13 years, Lynn has been a member of a quilting bee that trades blocks for scrap quilts. She loves scrap quilts because they give her the opportunity to use many different fabrics. She has had three of her quilts displayed at the IQA juried show in Houston, Texas—two of which were scrap quilts. Her first book, *Simple Strategies for Scrap Quilts* (Martingale & Company), was published in 2006. *Simple Strategies for Block-Swap Quilts* (Martingale & Company) was published in 2009.

Lynn currently lives in Houston, Texas, with her husband, an economics professor at Rice University. She and her husband have also lived in Pennsylvania, New Jersey, and New York. They have three grown children (Kim, Wes, and Nancy), one wonderful son-in-law (Craig), and two cherished grandchildren (Lillian and Eli). Lynn has been a seventh-grade science teacher and computer programmer. She received a kidney transplant in January of 2002, for which she is truly grateful.

THERE'S MORE ONLINE!

Discover more about Lynn and her quilts at www.LynnRoddyBrown.com. Find more great books on quilting at www.martingale-pub.com.